Sacred Unions

COWLEY PUBLICATIONS is a ministry of the brothers of the Society of Saint John the Evangelist, a monastic order in the Episcopal Church. Our mission is to provide books and resources for those seeking spiritual and theological formation. COWLEY PUBLICATIONS is committed to developing a new generation of writers and teachers who will encourage people to think and pray in new ways about spirituality, reconciliation, and the future.

Sacred Unions

A NEW GUIDE TO LIFELONG COMMITMENT

Thomas E. Breidenthal

Cowley Publications
CAMBRIDGE, MASSACHUSETTS

Published in the United States of America by Cowley Publications, a division of the Society of Saint John the Evangelist. No portion of this book may be reproduced, stored in or introduced into a retrieval system, or transmitted, in any form or by any means—including photocopying—without the prior written permission of Cowley Publications, except in the case of brief quotations embedded in critical articles and reviews.

Library of Congress Cataloging-in-Publication Data

Breidenthal, Thomas E., 1951–
    Sacred unions : a new guide to lifelong commitment / Thomas E. Breidenthal.
        p. cm.
    Includes bibliographical references.
      ISBN-10: 1-56101-249-1   ISBN-13: 0-978-156101-249-7
(pbk. : alk. paper)   1. Commitment (Psychology)—Religious aspects—Christianity.   2. Couples—Conduct of life.   3. Interpersonal relations—Religious aspects—Christianity.   I. Title.

BV4597.53.C56B74 2006
248.4—dc22

                                    2006003864

Scripture quotations are taken from the New Revised Standard Version of the Bible, © 1989, by the Division of Christian Education of the National Council of the Churches of Christ in the United States of America. Used by permission.

Cover design: Brad Norr Design
Interior design: Wendy Holdman

This book was printed in the United States of America on acid-free paper.

Cowley Publications
4 Brattle Street
Cambridge, Massachusetts 02138
800-225-1534 • www.cowley.org

To all true lovers

Contents

Acknowledgments

I am grateful to Cowley Publications for inviting me to write a book about lifelong unions that might speak to different-sex and same-sex couples alike. This task has stretched me, and that is always good. It has also renewed my old acquaintance with the literature of Christian romance and courtly love, about which I am especially glad. Thanks are due to my wife, Margaret, and our daughters, Magdalene and Lucy, for consenting to be the subject of various anecdotes, and, generally, for keeping me honest about marriage and household life. I also owe a debt of thanks to our friends Greg Harris and Marian Hyun, who were never far from my mind as I wrote this book. I am indebted to my executive assistant, Mona Villa-Sgobbo, who went out of her way to help me with technical difficulties. Finally, I want to acknowledge and thank my editor, Christy Risser-Milne, for providing the study questions and for challenging me with humor and grace.

Sacred Unions

ONE

Introduction
Sacred Unions

THIS BOOK IS A BOOK ABOUT TRUE LOVE. BY TRUE LOVE—
or romance—I mean sexual passion that deepens into the permanent union of two persons in heart, body, and mind. The reflec-
tions that follow are therefore addressed to all true lovers. Some of
you may be gay, some straight; some deep into the adventure of a
shared life, some just contemplating it; still others emerging out of
failure. I am hopeful that this discussion will speak to all these conditions, because I am convinced that the vision of lifelong union
is of central importance to everyone. It remains a viable option for
all of us, no matter who we are or what our story is. Some of the
challenges facing traditional and same-sex unions may be different,
but the essential disciplines and difficulties are the same. The path
of permanence is the same for everyone.

Permanence in Relationships

Why do we value permanence? From the romantic perspective the
answer is obvious. Falling in love is the same thing as yearning for
union. Initially, true love cannot abide any separation from its object. But as love grows and matures, we discover that this romantic
impulse is part of a more general human need for companionship. Our life and happiness depend on basic bonds that can be
counted on to be around for the long haul. The bond between two

people who join themselves together as life partners is one of these. Sometimes living out these relationships comes naturally, and we don't worry about why it is important to be there for each other. But when these relationships become strained, we begin to ask, "Is it worth it? Do I have to stick this out? What can I get out of this?"

At this point something like religion always kicks in. While there are many reasons to stick with a relationship that is demanding and difficult, two central ones are essentially religious. Either we work to preserve the relationship because we see this work as making us capable of greater happiness (fidelity and patience enlarge the soul), or we do so out of sheer obedience to the command to love the neighbor (my partner being the neighbor who is closest to me and whose claim is therefore greatest).

> Every other person is my neighbor, from the farthest away to the closest. I must love my partner first of all as a sister or brother for whom Christ died.

When all is said and done, these are also the real reasons for making a vow of lifelong fidelity in the first place. In my experience, most people who exchange such vows do so against the backdrop of some pretty intense coming-to-terms with their mortality, with the shape of their life as a whole. Every once in a while a couple will take issue with the final clause of the traditional marriage vow: "till death do us part." But I don't think this is because they haven't been thinking about death. They've been thinking about it a lot, because they are well aware that marriage itself is the kind of life-defining event that suddenly casts our whole journey from birth to death into high relief. This makes the rite's mention of death seem like the public exposure of a deeply private thought. But this private thought needs to be acknowledged and brought forward. To think about life with another is to contemplate the whole purpose of life from beginning to end, and so to frame that life within a larger purpose, whether that be a happiness that lies beyond material satisfaction, or a commitment to service that is constantly moving outward from the household into the world.

Religion and Relationship

None of this has to do with religion in the institutional sense. But it has everything to do with religion in its most basic sense, a sense that has largely been lost in our world where "religion" has become a word associated with abuse of power, exclusion, and rigidity of structure. To be religious is nothing more than being willing to pay attention to the claim of others whose self-interest may be different from our own. This is expressed beautifully in the New Testament's Letter of James: "Religion that is pure and undefiled before God, the Father, is this: to care for orphans and widows in their distress, and to keep oneself unstained from the world" (James 1:27). Religion is openness to others, and the willingness to be connected to them. This may well lead to openness to God (and vice versa), but God is not the sole focus of religion. The focus of religion is also the neighbor, that is, the other human being who stands before us. Because we know ourselves to be loved by God without qualification, we are able to surrender ourselves to God in trust. This same trust both enables and compels us to reach out to each other in love, sometimes out of a sense of profound obligation, sometimes out of the conviction that my happiness depends on finding my center outside myself. The religious disposition arises out of both the desire to serve and the desire to find true happiness; and in the end we find that both these desires turn out to be the same.

So to enter into a lifelong partnership is surely a religious act, since it involves just this kind of self-giving. When two people offer themselves to each other for life, they are witnessing to their belief that full human life is about service and other-centeredness.

They are making a faith statement that the fundamental rules that govern human life demand that we share everything we are and everything we have with others, and that genuine personal happiness lies in obeying that demand. I don't mean to imply that the exchange of vows primarily witnesses to a way of looking at the world, still less that our partners are merely representatives of every stranger that must be served—as if one person would do as well as another as the object of our self-giving. Of course not. When two people freely bestow themselves upon each other, they are not handing themselves over to just anyone. Each feels the call to cherish and serve *this* person, the yearning to be joined in every way possible with *this* person, the informed expectation that *this* person complements his or her own character in ways that will make for the creation of a household that works. I did not marry my wife in order to witness to any principle, but because I had fallen in love with her, and knew there was no one else I could imagine sharing my life with.

The Scandal of a Sacred Union

What I want us to notice is how remarkable it is that we should contemplate a lifetime together with someone, even though that someone attracts us in every way. Society no longer demands this of heterosexuals, and nearly everywhere puts barriers in the way of homosexual couples seeking to be together permanently. I suppose some new couples might delude themselves into thinking their future together is a fairy tale, but I doubt it: few people are foolish enough to think that the phrase "and they lived happily ever after" applies to them. But in over twenty years of premarital counseling, both in the church context and in the broader reach of ministry on a university campus, I have never once encountered a couple that did not genuinely intend and want to be joined until death. They were not naïve in this. They had watched couples struggling to juggle careers and conflicting job opportunities, with one spouse or the other usually having to make a career sacrifice for the sake of the other—and for the sake of the marriage. They had observed one partner absorbing the financial ruin of the other. They had seen faithful men and women devoting the better part of their lives to caring for a chronically sick partner. When I asked how they felt about exposing themselves to these burdens for the sake of staying together, they said that they would take them on willingly, because this was the right thing to do. Why was it the right thing to do? This is the answer I received over and over again from the couples themselves: We owe this kind of faithfulness and attention to each other not only because we have promised it, but simply because we depend on it as human beings handed over into each other's care.

In other words, the moral basis for fidelity in the face of hardship is love of neighbor. And if that is the moral principle that enjoins staying together, it must also be the moral principle that undergirds a couple's initial decision to be lifelong partners. All kinds of factors may draw a couple together in the first place, among them sexual attraction, personal compatibility, shared interests, dynastic ambitions, or economic advantages. But none of these factors accounts for the willingness, indeed, the desire, to stick it out even when any or all of these factors has ceased to be in play. What does account for it? Only a profound sense that the beloved, quite apart from his or her attractiveness, is another human being to be honored and cherished without qualification. To want to spend our whole lives with someone is a sign that we have already (perhaps even from the beginning) firmly planted our love in a moral terrain that includes sacrifice and loss.

I am not saying that everyone who seeks a lifelong union is religious, in the sense of being a member of an established religious community. I am simply saying that the impulse to lifelong fidelity is a sacrificial impulse, born of reverence for the beloved as someone who has value beyond his or her ability to satisfy my needs. This impulse is what religion comes down to in the end, and that is what a lifelong union comes down to, too. The decision to give oneself in mind, heart, and body to another person irrevocably, and the constant renewal of that commitment through time, is an essentially religious act that touches on all religious traditions, and includes couples who do not subscribe to any religious faith and may not even believe in God.

Christian Romanticism and True Love

This is the assumption that guides my attempt to lay out the challenges and disciplines of this kind of life together. As I said at the beginning, this book is about true love. But it might also be called a thought-experiment in the relationship of romance to the love of neighbor. With its roots in Christian mysticism and the medieval tradition of courtly love, Christian romanticism provides a way to think about sacred unions that embraces same-sex as well as heterosexual unions. Because romanticism means different things to different people, let me take a moment to clarify how I am using the term.

For some, romantic love is an unhelpful or even dangerous concept. Romantic love has been largely neglected by Church scholars, not because it has to do with sex but because it is regarded as not having *enough* to do with sex. In this view, the romantic sensibility leaps almost immediately from sexual passion to an idealized devotion that has little use for the body and still less use for humanity as a whole. In other words, romanticism is seen as the celebration of a relationship between two people who have turned their backs on the world.[1] This very negative take on romantic love has been used to disparage same-sex partnerships, the suggestion being that since homosexual love is not procreative, it is inherently selfish and antisocial. Romanticism has also been blamed for the high divorce rate in heterosexual partnerships. It is argued that if young couples were encouraged to focus less on romance and more on commitment and social responsibility, they would be less likely to separate when the romance fades.

I am taking a very different approach. As I will argue in coming chapters, there exists an authentic Christian romantic tradition, at the heart of which lies the conviction that sexual love can be a form of the love of neighbor. True love is born the moment sexual desire runs up against the vision of its object as a child of God. It is this epiphany—this deeper insight into each other's spiritual dignity and beauty—that sets two lovers on the road to union. And it is the deepening of this insight over time that continually inspires and renews the act of self-giving and the discipline of fidelity that make a union sacred.

The key phrase here is *over time.* It is the maturing of a relationship over many years that makes for holiness. Momentary fidelity is a contradiction in terms. It is faithfulness and steadfastness in the long haul that counts. Similarly, living together doesn't mean much until it bears fruit in the shared rhythms and common goals that transform a couple into a household. In the chapters that lie ahead, I will reflect on some of the challenges and opportunities inherent in this process of maturation and sanctification. Grounding my observations in an exploration of the roots of Christian romanticism, I will consider what goes into creating a household, how parenting can figure into the relationship, what to do when we hurt each other, and how we can survive the breakdown or the loss that comes with illness or death. Some of these topics will have more resonance for some than for others—not all of us are parents, and some of us have not experienced the loss of a partner. But I hope that the discussion as a whole will shed some light on how the adventure and the discipline of lifelong partnership trains us for the boundless fellowship we have in God.

What follows does not pretend to be an all-inclusive study of sacred unions. It is simply an invitation to learn more about ourselves as persons made for loving and for being loved. Obviously, I bring to this conversation my own faith commitment as a Christian. Indeed, the whole discussion will conclude with a consideration of what it means to be a committed partnership within the larger

Body of Christ. But since I believe the impulse to self-giving love stands at the heart of every great spiritual tradition, I hope that what follows will speak to many faiths. Perhaps W. H. Murray's words about commitment, which surely apply to the subject of this book, will apply to the book itself: "The moment one definitely commits oneself, then Providence moves too."

At the end of each chapter in this book is a set of questions and an exercise you and your partner may wish to consider engaging. These items may initially cause discomfort or a sense of "what does this have to do with us?" It is our hope that the action of engaging the questions and exercises openly and honestly will provide you with a fuller understanding of yourselves as individuals, a couple, and members of the Body of Christ.

TWO

True Love

And Who Is My Neighbor?

IN THE PREVIOUS CHAPTER, I SUGGESTED THAT TRUE ROMANTIC love is a form of the love of neighbor. In this chapter we will explore how this is so. But first let me be clear about what I mean by neighbor-love. In the biblical tradition, loving the neighbor means putting the interests and needs of other people ahead of one's own. Now this is a tricky idea, because it can so easily be misconstrued or misapplied. Putting other people first does not mean letting people who are going to hurt you get away with it. A fundamental tenet of Christian teaching is respect for oneself as a child of God. Another fundamental tenet is resisting evil. So putting other people first does not mean putting oneself down. Still less does it mean inviting or condoning mistreatment of oneself by others. Neighbor-love must always include insisting that the neighbor claim his or her dignity as a child of God, and acting accordingly. Putting the neighbor's interests ahead of my own means overcoming my own selfishness and self-centeredness so that I become free to love responsibly and fearlessly. It means being so certain of my worth as someone for whom Christ died that I will risk the loss of status or privilege to stand with the weak and the despised. Putting the needs of the other first has nothing to do with putting up with abuse: it opposes it in every way.

Love of neighbor also involves treating everyone with the same respect: whoever crosses my path has a claim on my love, whether he is a beggar or a prince. In other words, I am not to measure out my love in proportion to the other person's ability to benefit me in return, since the point is to place my own interests to one side. So the word *neighbor* comes to signify any other human being who happens to be standing before me or who is present to my consciousness. By the same token, because neighbor-love does not make distinctions between people as to their worth or usefulness, loving one's neighbor implies a readiness to love *every* neighbor. Thus, *neighbor* can mean the human race as a whole, regarded as a collection of people, all of whom are potential and deserving recipients of my love.

Unfortunately, this can and does lead to the word's use as a generic term—as if the neighbor were simply everybody else besides me, lumped under one heading without distinction. But it is impossible for neighbor-love to overlook the differences among people. When we set our own self-interest aside, we also withdraw the categories we had used to sort people out according to their usefulness. Love does not replace those categories with new ones; still less does it impose a universal category marked simply "not self." But when love beholds another person, it sees without an agenda, and so *really* sees who *this* person uniquely is. At the same time, it sees him against the background of countless other neighbors in all *their* distinctiveness.

Finally, love of neighbor is just one step away from the love of God. Jesus brings their proximity into sharp focus when he brings Deuteronomy 6:5 ("Love God with all your heart") and Leviticus 19:18 ("Love your neighbor as yourself") together in order to summarize the Jewish law (Matthew 22:37–40). The love of God naturally leads to the love of neighbor because every human being is the object of God's love: if we are to love God, we must love our neighbors and ourselves, too. But it works in the other direction also. To see another person as she really is, with our vision unclouded by prejudice and projection, is to recognize the existence of someone who is both related to me (we are both members of the human race) and completely outside of me and beyond me. This is to discover the neighbor as elusive and unknowable, ultimately indefinable by my will or my story. This is very much like the experience of encountering God, and indeed often goes hand in hand with it. The same clarity of vision that reveals the neighbor as unknowable can open my eyes to the absolute otherness of God. Just as discovering the neighbor calls into question all my attempts to absorb or annex other people into my life, so discovering God unbalances and decenters me, forcing me to recognize that the world revolves around God, not me. The two experiences are practically interchangeable.

The Hebrew Scriptures play on the fine line that separates encounter with the neighbor from encounter with God. At crucial moments in the narrative, texts suggest that encounters with the divine can easily masquerade as encounters with the neighbor, and vice versa. When Abraham and Sarah show hospitality to three mysterious strangers, it is unclear whether they are angels or men (Genesis 18:1–15)—Christian tradition has sometimes identified them with the Holy Trinity. When Jacob wrestles all night with someone who leaves him with a limp and a new name (Israel), his attacker could be an angel, a man, or God (Genesis 32:24–32). When the angel of the Lord visits Samson's parents to foretell his birth, they think he is simply a "man of God," until he ascends back into heaven with the smoke of their burnt offering (Judges 13:2–20).

The entire prophetic tradition can be read as a study in the uncertain frontier that divides human witness from divine revelation. Hosea marries a prostitute and God's inextinguishable love for Israel is demonstrated (Hosea 1–14). Ezekiel starves himself in anguish over the direction of government policy, and the starvation of Jerusalem under siege is foretold (Ezekiel 4:9–13).

For the purposes of this discussion, one of the most interesting illustrations of the analogy of God and neighbor is the Song of Songs (or Song of Solomon). This is a highly erotic dialogue between a woman and a man, expressing their love for each other and their desire to have sex. The book owes its place in the Jewish canon to the fact that, at some point, it began to be read as an allegory of the relationship of God and Israel. But the love poem could only function in this way if it were understood that the relationship of self to neighbor (which includes that of lover to lover) is analogous to the relationship of self to God.

Jesus: Neighbor and God

This analogy of the relationship of neighbor to God takes center-stage in the New Testament, with the Gospels' portrayal of Jesus as both God and human being. In all four Gospels, this portrayal hinges on the conjunction of the divine and the human in the neighbor. The key here is Jesus' identification of himself with the Son of Man, a mysterious figure in the Book of Daniel who is sent from the throne of God to establish justice on earth (Daniel 7:13–14). This figure seems to be both divine and human. He is seen by Daniel coming "with the clouds of heaven," but he looks like a human being (a son of man). He is presented to God (it is unclear whether this happens before or after his coming on the clouds), and emerges from this audience with what seems like divine power to rule the earth (Daniel 7:13–14). So when Jesus calls himself the Son of Man, he is drawing attention to his own ambiguous status and pedigree. "Son of Man" can refer specifically to the figure foretold in Daniel (itself ambiguous), or it can be taken as a reference to any typical human being ("Everyman"). This could be interpreted as a way to keep us in suspense about who and what Jesus really is, but I don't think that's right. Jesus is being presented to us in the Gospels as the meeting point of God and humankind, and he is that meeting point precisely because he is a neighbor to each of us.

Thus, within the Christian tradition, loving Jesus—having a personal relationship with Christ—becomes the paradigm for the love of neighbor. Of course, loving Jesus is no replacement for our obligation to love every neighbor. Jesus' efficacy as redeemer lies partly in his ability to shake us out of our self-absorption and make

Let him kiss me with the kisses of his mouth!
For your love is better than wine,
> your anointing oils are fragrant. (Song of Songs 1:2–3)

So begins the Song of Songs, a book of the Bible that is unashamed in its celebration of sexual desire. Here are a few examples of its highly-charged erotic imagery:

My beloved is to me a bag of myrrh
> that lies between my breasts.
My beloved is to me a cluster of henna blossoms
> in the vineyards of En-gedi (1:13–14).

How fair and pleasant you are,
> O loved one, delectable maiden!
You are stately as a palm tree,
> and your breasts are like its clusters.
I say I will climb the palm tree
> and lay hold of its branches (7:6–8).

The imagery of the Song may strike the modern reader as excessive, to the point of ceasing to be erotic:

Your neck is like an ivory tower.
Your eyes are pools in Heshbon,
> by the gate of Bath-rabbin.
Your nose is like a tower of Lebanon,
> overlooking Damascus. (7:4)

The point is that the beloved so fills the imagination of the lover that every aspect of the environment is saturated with the beloved's presence, and vice versa.

us see him. Once we see him—and love him—he helps us see all the other neighbors who require our love. Or so it should be.

Christianity's Struggles with a Simple Command

Over its long history, Christian teaching has not always taken at face value Jesus' command that we should love one another as he has loved us. We must not forget that Gentile Christianity was incubated within the cultural matrix of the late Roman Empire, an intellectual environment that denigrated human relationships— marriage, parenthood, friendship, excessive concern for the chance stranger—as obstacles standing in the way of spiritual advance- ment. This predisposition to value solitude over community is summed up very well in a tag from Plotinus, one of the great phi- losophers of the time, who approvingly described the soul's jour- ney toward God as "the flight of the alone to the Alone."

This distrust of connection to others was challenged head-on by the biblical command to love the neighbor, but it also had a corro- sive effect on it. When the great North African bishop, Augustine of Hippo, was still a fairly new Christian, he argued that loving the neighbor meant feeding and clothing him—and keeping him at arm's length so as not to distract him from his eternal salvation! In his old age Augustine arrived at a very different understanding, envisioning heaven as an endless occasion for enjoying sweet com- munion with countless other fellow citizens of the kingdom of God.[2] This reversal was the hard-won fruit of his own deep en- gagement with the Bible's affirmation of community, but it would be centuries before his breakthrough would be taken up by the Church. This work began in the early years of the first millennium, and it picked up steam in the twelfth and thirteenth centuries. The work proceeded on two fronts: rediscovering that devotion to Jesus propels us toward the neighbor, not away from him, and acknowl- edging that any encounter with the other as neighbor is of spiritual significance, with or without the mediation of Jesus.

The Example of St. Francis

Francis of Assisi (1181–1226 CE) provides the most vivid example of this reversal. The direction of his life can be plotted by three events. First, his journey as a saint begins when Christ speaks to him from a cross in a local church. From then on Francis would emphasize devotion to the humanity of Jesus, crucified and risen, thus reintroducing into Christian piety a relationship to Jesus as neighbor that we take for granted, but that had been virtually forgotten for centuries. Second, Francis's whole ministry is defined by his decision to embrace a leper whom he encountered on the road. This act was a direct consequence of his rediscovery of Jesus as neighbor. Francis realized that devotion to the humanity of Jesus required devotion to every human being, including the most repellent. This embrace became the touchstone of the Franciscan movement, which required the "little brothers" to live as homeless beggars among the general populace in order to maximize contact with the neighbor. The third and final event is Francis's receiving the stigmata, the actual wounds of Christ, in his own body. This seals Francis's total union with Christ, but, significantly, the union is with Christ crucified and risen. Again, the humanity of Jesus is in the forefront. The gift of the stigmata demonstrates that Francis has truly imitated Jesus the neighbor in his care for all neighbors. Francis aroused the imagination of the Christian community with the vision of a Christian life completely dedicated to the love of neighbor. But the Franciscan way was a way of self-denial. The followers of Francis avoided particular attachments so that they could be available to everybody.

The Troubadours and Christian Romanticism

I would now like to turn our attention to a parallel development that speaks to the topic of this book, the sacred union of two people in heart, mind, and body. About the same time Francis was establishing his order, refined reflection on sexual passion and love was emerging as a major literary theme, primarily among the troubadours, or court poets, of Provence, in what is now southern France. (It is possible that Francis himself had contact with troubadours in his youth, and aspired to become one. His own skill as a poet is evident from the spiritual canticles that he wrote as an adult.) This

Troubador poetry combined highly erotic imagery with rich spiritual content. Here is a sestina by one of the greatest poets in this tradition, Arnaut Daniel, who flourished in the twelfth century. Here the longed for sexual union borrows heavily from religious imagery.

The Firm Desire
Translated by Garrick Davis

I have a firm desire, and I enter
Unbending, driven deeply, hard as nail.
What lies! Such gossip has plundered my soul—
But since I cannot bear this flimsy rod,
I'll play the flute until it cries uncle
In secret, before her closet-chamber.

I go softly limp before that chamber
Where conquering men can never enter;
The bedroom guard, both angels and uncles,
Dissolve pride—even to the fingernails—
Of suitors, stiff like boys before the rod.
Such fears of not being hers, in my soul!

At least in bodied flesh, if not in soul,
Let her hide me, once, in that chamber!
Let wounds the heart embraced not spare the rod!
Servant to her secrets, I should enter!
Now bind me close to her—as flesh to nail—
And heed no warnings from friend or uncle.

literary development would eventually give rise to the courtly love tradition in European literature.

The origins of this movement are murky. In the eleventh and twelfth centuries, southern France had become a powerful strong-hold of the Cathari, a spiritual movement that emphasized purity and self-denial, and rejected the material world and sexuality as

Even the sweet daughter of my uncle
I never loved so well—with all my soul.
The quick between her finger and her nail,
So would I be, and press into her chamber.
And molded to its will, love would enter
This heart, this soldier with a tender rod.

Since syrup last flowed from a withered rod,
And Adam fathered nephew and uncle,
Never has love blossomed so! Now enter
My heart, and dwell in neither flesh nor soul,
But where she lives—in each street, each chamber
That bears me, Father, to the Sacred Nail.

At last, veil bloodied by the caulking nail!
My heart holds her, as bark to sapling-rod.
My dizzying tower's joy, her chamber
Where no love for father, friend, or uncle
Remains—only Heaven's sweet-doubled soul
In spooning's cup, where I slowly enter.

Arnaut spouts song of nail crying, "uncle!"
By grace of her who claims the rod's bent soul,
To all! Unchamber her praise, and enter!

evils to be escaped. Ironically, it was in this environment that the troubadours—and their love songs—first flourished. Were the poets simply appropriating sexual imagery to a spirituality of solitude (and thus negating real sexual relations)? Perhaps. If so, this would parallel the simultaneous re-emergence in Christian circles of a theological tradition that focused on the soul's marriage to Christ while devaluing earthly marriage as unspiritual because it was sexual.

Or were they engaged in subverting the Catharist ideology? If so, they would have presented a challenge for the Christian authorities as well. Even though the Christian establishment rejected the Cathari as heretics, and carried out a brutal crusade to destroy them, the Catharist rejection of the body was hardly more than an exaggeration of Christianity's own tendencies in the West. So if the troubadours were championing erotic love, they were challenging the drift of western theology up to that point.

My own view is that their movement was a deeply Christian celebration of chaste sexual love, which took the ancient Christian notion of the soul's marriage to Christ and read it back into the sphere of the erotic.[3]

Troubadour means "finder." The term is usually taken to refer to these poets' skill in finding just the right combination of diction, meter, and rhyme to match their subject. But they can also be credited with finding a new way to understand sexual union. What they discovered and celebrated was a passion that, although it did not exclude sexual satisfaction, sought to offer itself in service and devotion to the beloved. Since it was not long before protestations of this sort were viewed as a classic strategy for seduction, it is hard to appreciate the original freshness and sincerity of this subordination of sexual desire to respect. The troubadours were expropriating erotic religious imagery in order to celebrate the spiritual value of faithful sexual love.

The Bible Erotic

This is quite evident if we consider the three chief elements of the romantic sensibility: extravagant praise of the beloved's qualities, an attitude of humble service to the beloved, and the hope of actual union with the beloved. These elements reflect a self-conscious return to and re-appropriation of the three biblical texts that combine in the mystical tradition to produce the theme of the soul's union with Christ. These texts are the Song of Songs, Ephesians 5:25–33, and Revelation 21:2.

Ephesians 5:25–33 lays out the duties of husbands to wives. It assumes a patriarchal system that places men over women. However, by insisting that the model for authority is Christ's love for the Church, this passage implies that men should give up their privilege, just as Christ gave up his life on the cross: "Husbands, love your wives, just as Christ loved the church and gave himself up for her."

Revelation 21:2 pictures the fulfillment of God's purpose for humankind as a marriage between Jesus and a new and purified Jerusalem: "I saw the holy city, the new Jerusalem, coming down out of heaven from God, prepared as a bride adorned for her husband." What is foreseen is complete fellowship between humankind and God.

As we saw earlier, the Song of Songs is a sequence of passionate love poems addressed by a man and a woman to each other. By the time Christians were reflecting on it, it was already regarded by the rabbis as a window onto the love affair of God and Israel. It was not long before Christian theologians were applying it to the relationship between Christ and his Church. They were encouraged in this by Ephesians 5:25–33, which compares the good husband to Christ, who gave up his life for the Church, and the conclusion of Revelation, which looks forward to the wedding day of the Lamb (Christ) with the new Jerusalem (the Church). Although these texts were viewed as being primarily about the Church as a whole, they were also applied to the individual soul, enraptured with love of Christ, experiencing Christ's courtship and self-sacrificing lordship, and waiting to be united with him on the other side of Good Friday.

The notion of the soul as the bride of Christ was re-emerging as a major theme in Christian mystical theology just as the concept of courtly love was taking shape. It is hard to say which came first, or if either caused the other. Either way, the dynamic of courtly love clearly tapped into the old notion of the soul's relationship with Christ. It did so, however, by turning the tables and identifying the lover with Christ and the beloved with the soul. It would be easy to overlook the significance of this reversal. The troubadours were men giving voice to their love for real (or imagined) women. We should not be surprised, then, that when their poetry taps into the erotic imagery of Christian mysticism, the speaker assumes a role analogous to that of Christ. But this is precisely what is so remarkable. In order to appropriate the mystical tradition in the service of earthly, sexual love, the troubadours reread Ephesians 5:25–33 as if it were addressed to them as men who love women rather than souls beloved of Christ. What this means, in effect, is that, in the very act of creating a sensibility that celebrates sexual union, they discover in the object of their desire the neighbor, someone for whom Christ died. After all, the reference to loving one's wife as one loves one's own body is a direct reference to the Levitical command: you shall love your neighbor as yourself (Leviticus 19:18). If we needed scriptural support for the claim that sexual love can be a vehicle for the love of neighbor, this is it.

In any case, the troubadours' appropriation of Ephesians 5:25–33 as a passage addressed directly to them shapes the romantic tradition from the outset. As I suggested above, the three motifs that together define the romantic tradition—reverence for the beloved, submission to the beloved, and hope of permanent union with the beloved—are immediately traceable to Ephesians. The exaltation of the beloved in the lover's eyes is nothing other than wonder and respect in the face of the beloved revealed as neighbor. The lover's desire to do her bidding is at once an acknowledgment of the neighbor's authority and an imitation of Christ's own servant ministry. The lover's yearning to be united bodily and spiritually to the beloved is a reflection of Christ's own union with his Church.

The Example of Dante

It would be a mistake to interpret these modulations of the Ephesians passage as a parody of it. When it is true to its original genius, the romantic tradition is a serious and high-minded exploration of the conjunction of sexual love and Christian love. But of course the tradition has its false imitators. It is very easy to slip from the exaltation of the beloved as neighbor to the idolization of the beloved as the ultimate object of desire, to the exclusion of all other neighbors and even of God. When this happens, love of neighbor falls away; the beloved is lost sight of as a neighbor, and becomes merely the projection of the lover's own needs. This approach to love was criticized early on from within the romantic tradition as being fundamentally un-Christian—most notably by Dante in his *Divine Comedy,* where he finds two lovers obsessed with lust for each other condemned to whirl endlessly in each other's arms around the outer circle of hell (*Inferno* 5:73–142). Dante's description makes it clear that, despite their eternal embrace, in turning their backs on God and the neighbor, they have lost each other as well. Most significantly, he blames their demise on reading the story of Lancelot's love for Guinevere—apparently an example of the wrong kind of romance!

True love in the romantic tradition is well illustrated by Dante's approach to his own beloved Beatrice. Obsessed with her from a distance as a young man, Dante is prevented by her early death from ever attaining her. His first great work is a series of poems that both tell the story of his love and chronicle how he manages, at last, to accept that Beatrice could never be the sole object of his love: to honor her goodness he must also honor God, and both are truly accomplished if she is acknowledged as a fellow creature of God. In other words, Dante must learn to love her as his neighbor. The result of this recontextualization of his love is *The Divine Comedy,* in which Beatrice reappears as the saintly guide who leads him up through the spheres of heaven to the vision of God.

On the face of it, Dante's way of relating romantic love to the love of neighbor does not have much to do with ordinary life. He never has sex with Beatrice, and their reunion takes place in heaven, when sex is no longer an issue. This failure to consummate a sexual union is not uncommon in the romantic tradition, especially early on. So it is fair to ask whether this tradition really is about sexual union after all, or whether it is just one more way to devalue sex as unspiritual and base.

I am inclined to reject the second option, for the following reasons. First, if, as I see it, the romantic sensibility is grounded in scripture, then it is grounded in a worldview that affirms human sexuality as a dimension of our nature as created by God. Second, if romanticism arises out of the discovery that the object of sexual love is first and foremost our neighbor, it should come as no surprise that the tradition spends a considerable period of time reeling from—as well as reveling in—that finding. Wonder in the face of the beloved-as-neighbor might well inspire a sense of unworthiness for sexual union in the heart of the lover. If that is the case, what we see in the endless postponements and sublimations typical of romance is not the denigration of sexual love, but great respect for it.

Edmund Spenser: Sacred Romance

At any rate, as the romantic tradition develops and matures, it becomes increasingly clear that its core value is the affirmation of sexual

Edmund Spenser (1552–1599) was a contemporary of Shakespeare and shares his greatness as a poet. A devout Christian who aspired to write poetry worthy of Elizabethan England's highest aspirations, Spenser was an ardent supporter of the English Reformation who believed strongly that every layperson was called to take his or her faith seriously and to strive for sanctity. His book-length poem *The Faerie Queene* is actually a rich tangle of stories about various knights and ladies (including one woman who is a knight), each of which represents a virtue necessary for the Christian life. For instance, Book 1, about the virtue of holiness, is the story of a bumbling young knight who constantly lets down his beloved Una. Eventually, Una rescues him from suicidal despair, and he emerges as a chastened but powerful witness to the power of love. He turns out to be St. George, and the climax of Book 1 is a battle with the Dragon of panoramic scope, followed by marriage to Una. Spenser's epic poem is important for this book because it is the greatest example in the English language of the Christian romantic tradition. The story of St. George centers on his romantic relationship with Una—indeed, the way Spenser casts this saint's journey to spiritual victory perfectly illustrates how this tradition fuses Christ's love for the soul and the soul's love for God with the union of two persons in body, mind, and heart. It is all the more pertinent that Spenser places such an extraordinarily high value on marriage, which he clearly views as the highest possible spiritual path. It is no accident that St. George's story culminates in marriage.

union as a form of neighbor-love. An obvious example of this in the English-speaking world is the Elizabethan poet Edmund Spenser, whose entire career, from his beautiful *Epithalamion,* written on the occasion of his own marriage, to his epic poem *The Faerie Queene,* celebrates the dignity of lifelong sexual union in countless ways. Of course, Spenser was writing as a child of the Reformation, in an age actively engaged in elevating marriage to a status equal to or higher than celibacy. But the romantic tradition was a ready resource in the pursuit of that agenda, because all along it had harbored the dream of a love in which reverence and sexual union would go hand in hand.

In short, the romantic tradition demonstrates how art informs theology, and vice versa. And just as the romantic tradition helped the Christian world rediscover the marriage of man and woman as a spiritual vocation, so now, as we struggle to extend our understanding of that vocation to include partners of the same sex, that tradition emerges once again as a fruitful starting point and a rich resource for that discussion. For although Ephesians 5:25–33, to which the romantic vision continues to direct us, is about men loving women, once the principle is established that sexual love can and should be a form of neighbor-love, it follows that what defines the beloved as worthy of reverence is not his or her gender in relation to my own, but his or her status as neighbor, relative to my obligation to serve the neighbor. Otherwise we would have to conclude that men have a monopoly on the imitation of Christ, at least when it comes to sexual unions. But I cannot accept such a conclusion. Having exhorted wives to submit to their husbands, the author of Ephesians proceeds in a roundabout but ultimately very effective manner to tell husbands to do the same. By the end of the passage, it is clear that the authority of the husband is nothing more than the authority of the crucified Christ, who is servant of all. By the same token, it is clear that the original exhortation to submission on the woman's part must also be rethought. To submit to the husband as if he were Christ on the cross is to submit to him as if he were Christ the neighbor.

So when all is said and done, the wife is to honor her husband as her neighbor, just as the husband is to honor his wife as *his* neighbor. In the end then, the two submissions are the same: both husband and wife receive each other's love (as the Church receives Christ's love), and both pour out their lives for the other (as Christ pours out his life for the Church). Indeed, since the author of Ephesians calls the Church Christ's Body—which is to say that it is Christ's *self*—we can say that, just as the Church loves Jesus back by being Christ to him, so the wife loves her husband back by being Christ to *him.* So both are neighbor, and both are imitators of Christ. It is not a question, then, of male and female. Inasmuch as sexual union is holy, its holiness resides in the initiative each partner takes in laying his or her life down for the other by promising lifelong fidelity.

Gender in Romance

Gender also turns out to be of secondary importance in the romantic tradition. As we have seen, the tradition is born when male poets place their love lyrics under the authority of Ephesians. But once it is established that sexual love and love of neighbor go together, it becomes clear that the romantic sensibility is not a male preserve. In Book 1 of Spenser's *Faerie Queene,* the beautiful and righteous Una is an allegory of the Church, while the Redcross Knight (who turns out to be St. George), becomes, by fits and starts, an allegory of Christ. But even though Spenser's account of their relationship clearly situates it within the orbit of Ephesians 5:25–33, it is Una, not Redcross, who functions as faithful lover, and who manages to guide Redcross to sainthood, despite his infidelities and weaknesses. Again, if we confined ourselves to literature in the English language, it would be difficult to list all the literary works since Spenser in which women function primarily in the role of lover, rather in the role of the beloved. We need think only of Jane in *Jane Eyre* and Dorothea in *Middlemarch.*

But if gender roles are interchangeable in the romantic tradition, they are also immaterial. I am not talking about sexual orientation here, but about the motifs of reverence, service, and expectation that define the dynamics of romance. A story line about two men or two women is able to sound these motifs as completely as one about a man and a woman, as the subplot about the two male lovers in the 1994 British film *Four Weddings and a Funeral* amply demonstrates. In this movie, a young group of university graduates support one another as they come of age, and some of them marry. Meanwhile, the main protagonists (played by Andie MacDowell and Hugh Grant) pursue an extremely highly-charged and uncertain relationship, which culminates in lifelong commitment, but not formal marriage. In ironic contrast to all these couples stand Gareth and Matthew—completely stable and committed, yet (one supposes) desiring the legal status that comes with formal marriage, if only that were available to them. After Gareth's heart failure and death, Matthew quotes W. H. Auden's romantic elegy:

> He was my North, my South, my East, my West,
> My working week and my Sunday rest,
> My noon, my midnight, my talk, my song:
> I thought love would last forever: I was wrong.
>
> The stars are not wanted now: put out every one;
> Pack up the moon and dismantle the sun;
> Pour out the ocean and sweep up the wood;
> For nothing now can ever come to any good.[4]

Loving All Our Neighbors

One question remains regarding the romantic tradition. I have claimed that the romantic tradition takes its bearings from the discovery that sexual love can and should be neighbor-love. That seems to be true as far as the lover's love for the beloved goes. But as I suggested early on in this chapter, the love of one neighbor implies the love of all neighbors. Is the romantic tradition capable of following the logic of neighbor-love to this conclusion? I think there is no doubt that it is.

George Eliot's great Victorian novel *Middlemarch* can be read as a thought-experiment about this very question. The novel turns on Dorothea's love for Will Ladislaw, whom she eventually marries after the death of her unloving but endlessly needy first husband. Dorothea's passion for Will is unbounded, but by this point in her life, it is very certain that she cannot give herself to a relationship that will not also further empower her to make a difference for good in the world. Her marriage to Will must (and in the novel does) widen the horizon of service, not narrow it. What George Eliot is getting at in *Middlemarch* is "true love," that is, sexual passion that has been imbued with the love of God and neighbor, so that it is not only sexual but also faithful (as in *troth,* fidelity) and truth-seeking. It is precisely the passion for truth embedded in true love that constantly compels true lovers to look beyond themselves, and to extend their care for each other to more and more people, in ever-widening circles.

Dorothea's ardor, likened by George Eliot to that of St. Teresa of Ávila, may well bring out the romantic tradition's inherent commitment to care for every neighbor. But, like any account of heroic love, it calls our own commitments into question. Is it too idealistic to call sexual love to the standards of neighbor-love—especially a love of neighbor that extends beyond commitment to one's own partner and immediate family? This may seem counterintuitive, even to religious people, since it seems to demand that lovers, at the very height of their movement toward each other, pull back from each other and see past each other to something more general. But this is a false problem.

To fall in love is to stumble across the person who at one and the same time captivates us with his or her beauty—be it physical or spiritual—and deflects our love outward toward others. True love makes us more alive to the world, more eager to serve the stranger, more open to the risk of neighbor-love. It is exactly analogous to what the great mystics say about turning toward God: one is immediately filled with new energy for service. What makes us want to spend our life with someone is precisely this: that the sexual attraction opens up almost immediately onto a wider horizon, or is itself produced and shaped by that horizon. There is no place for simply having one's needs met, because those needs are no longer of central importance.

In other words, union with one person is a kind of down payment on union with everyone else. I can approach my union with another in such a way that it exposes me to the challenge of universal fellowship rather than shielding me from it. At the most basic level, this means embracing fellowship with my partner's family and friends. But it also means taking in the full reality of my partner's relationships and struggles in the workplace.

My wife, Margaret, and I share our experiences at work every day. The temptation is to use these conversations to bring closure to the day—as if we could set our work relationships to one side, and get back to *us*. But sometimes, by God's grace, each of us finds his or her heart drawn into the dynamic of the other's workplace. So I end up worrying daily about a volunteer at Margaret's place who is grieving the loss of his life-partner, and Margaret is asking for updates about how a staff member's child is doing in college. We tend to take these natural extensions of our sphere of care for granted, but they are important. And they are a sign that our relationship is not a defense against the world, but a further entry into it. It often happens that couples are able to reach out to others in ways that would have been impossible for either of them singly. I have seen couples transform a parish community simply by virtue of their hospitality to friend and stranger alike. It all comes down to how we as couples perceive ourselves. Are we joined together in solidarity *against* the world, or is our joining the beginning of a shared journey into the world of humankind?

Embracing the world together is not as easy as it sounds. It requires a commitment to something that transcends the relationship. We must both accept that the neighbors we run up against in our own work are a responsibility we share. This means that our union is not a refuge, but a source of constant exposure for each of us. It also means that we are confronted each day by the fact that, however much our lives are intertwined, they are not the same life. Each of us brings different concerns to the dinner table very evening, and this is because, most of the time, we are out there on our own, dealing with conflict, covering for a sick colleague, assuaging someone's grief. So we are constantly reminded that our paths, our vocations, our ministries are not the same. To open ourselves to the world is therefore to acknowledge the space that the world opens between us.

How can I allow this opening to take place? I must see my beloved as having an ultimate destiny that has a wider reach than her relationship with me. I must try to see her for who she is, quite apart from those aspects of her that attract me, and quite apart from the romanticized composite image I have of her as the answer to all my needs and lacks. I have to be sure, in other words, that when I surrender myself to her, I am not really just handing myself over to a projection of myself to a rescuer whose job it is to make everything all right in my life. And that's not all. To look on her as my neighbor is to acknowledge the claim of every neighbor to my attention. So, as I work out my neighborly relationship with my wife, I realize that she is, if you will, a stand-in for everyone else, as well as the particular neighbor who is teaching me, throughout a lifetime of ups and downs, how to stop putting myself first.

1. What do you think of this notion of true love being based in the command to love your neighbor? How does it affect your perspective on your partner? On the world around you?
2. Ephesians 5:22–33 has long been interpreted to keep women "in their place." How does the interpretation put forward here change your view? How do you integrate this positively into your life as a couple?
3. How has your love for your partner broadened your ability to love others?

Exercise:

Read the Song of Songs out loud together. (Use the NRSV or the Jewish Publication Society's TANAKH translation if possible.) Reflect together on the passion the lovers have for each other. How do you see these feelings reflected in your feelings for each other? Treat this as an opportunity to be completely open and honest about the sensuality of your relationship. Western culture frowns on this sort of expression. Put that aside and discover within yourself and your partner a healthy sensuality that strengthens your relationship to each other, and thus strengthens your relationship to your neighbors and to God.

THREE

The Act of Self-Giving

I HAVE DEFINED TRUE LOVE AS SEXUAL DESIRE CONJOINED with love of God and neighbor. What does such love entail? Since love of God is implicit in the love of neighbor (and vice versa), I will only address myself to neighbor-love at this point. Loving the neighbor means putting the neighbor first. Thus Paul, urging the Philippians to have "the same love," encourages them: "Do nothing from selfish ambition or conceit, but in humility regard others as better than yourselves" (Philippians 2:3). This does not mean silencing ourselves or denying our own dignity. Paul is enjoining those who know themselves to be loved by God to exercise the discipline of humility. Humility is not a denial of our own dignity as children of God. It is the practice whereby we recognize that others besides us are also God's children. When Paul suggests that we regard others as better than ourselves, he is not saying that we are to devalue ourselves. He is saying, rather, that we must make an effort to take the neighbor seriously as a fellow recipient of God's love. When we view ourselves in a position of privilege, this will require that we engage in a thought-experiment: "This neighbor who has less worldly privilege than I have is better in God's eyes than I am." But then the reverse must also be true. When I have been rejected or oppressed by my neighbor, I may not need to consider him or her better than I am, but I still need to rejoice if that person is a recipient of God's love along with me.

But what does it mean to suggest that this kind of humility can go hand in hand with sexual desire? Such is our culture's ambivalence about sex that it sometimes finds it difficult to imagine these two things going together. We tend to suppose that our age has made its peace with sexuality, or has embraced it unreservedly. Certainly we are permissive about sex. Certainly we glamorize it. Sometimes we glorify it. But we are by no means free of the prejudice inherited by Christianity from late Greco-Roman culture, that sexual desire is by nature selfish, and perhaps even essentially violent.

Britomart's Journey

There is a scene in Book 3 of Spenser's *Faerie Queene* in which Britomart, the woman knight who will ultimately exemplify chastity or Christian sexual love, enters the house of a magician who is trying to remove the heart of Amoret. His intent is to thwart true love, symbolized in this case by the faithful Amoret, whose heart belongs to her beloved Scudamour. The magician's name is Busirane, which is a reference to abuse. He is aptly named, for in attempting to remove Amoret's heart, he is not only committing an act of violence against her but also taking advantage of her capacity for love. If Amoret's heart had not been extended to Scudamour, it would not be so available to Busirane. (This is what abusers always count on: the love of the child for the parent, his or her trust of relatives and family friends; love of God expressed in devotion to the pastor. The dangers of opening one's heart to anyone are such that one might consider opening one's heart to no one.) This is precisely the challenge that faces Britomart. It is Britomart's duty and desire to rescue Amoret, but she is not so sure that sexual desire is a good thing. She cannot rescue Amoret until she faces her own ambivalence about sexuality. She wants to engage in the love of neighbor that can be the substance and the fruit of a lifelong union, but she fears the exposure to abuse that this involves. Spenser dramatizes this inner struggle by depicting the first room of Busirane's house as a vast gallery of paintings depicting story after story, myth after myth of seduction and rape. Britomart manages to advance from the first room into the second, only to witness there a staged pageant in which all the miseries and vices associated with sexual adventure are portrayed in gruesome detail. She is terrified, but her concern for Amoret keeps her from retreating, and she finally breaks into the inner room and rescues her.[5]

My point is that Britomart's confusion about sex anticipates our confusion. We, too, labor under the misconception that sexual desire and genuine affection don't mix. They may well coexist in our hearts, but they cannot both be switched on at the same time. Spenser's great poem about Christian romance rejects this out of hand. Building on the foundation laid by the troubadours, and adding in his own Reformation conviction that marriage is a high road to sanctification, Spenser reminds us that sexualized violence has nothing to do with sexual desire. For Spenser, sex is essentially nonviolent. Far from being rooted in the impulse to dominate and control, sexual desire finds its most authentic expression in yielding and letting go.

Certainly, the anguish of unrealized sexual union can easily lead to the kind of persistent and dogged pursuit that borders on the aggressive. But this is what ethicists call a "limit situation"—an extreme example that doesn't tell us much about the moral terrain we are traversing in ordinary life. Spenser is inviting us to consider what sexual desire feels like when ordinary people experience it, and what kind of behavior it gives rise to when it is coupled with a reasonable amount of discipline and maturity. His own conclusion, which I agree with, is that sexual desire is a form of suffering (remember that passion means suffering). It is a form of suffering because we are not in control of its satisfaction. The lover is entirely dependent on the response of the beloved. That is why sexual passion—when it does not degenerate into a general hunger for sex with anyone, anywhere, anyhow—can provide a powerful and effective schooling in humility and patience.

Even when passion finds its consummation in sexual union, there is a certain suffering that accompanies the joy, whether it be the anxiety or shame of self-exposure, a lingering lack of trust in one's partner, or the sheer pain of losing complete control over one's own body and one's life. Spenser brings all this out. Patience and endurance are exhibited in Amoret's courageous refusal to escape further torture by giving Busirane her heart. In turn, her courage is a turning point for Britomart. When Britomart enters the inner room, she sees living proof that sexual passion can go hand in hand with faithful witness in the face of persecution. In the end, this encounter helps Britomart accept her own sexuality as compatible with nobility and virtue, and prepares her for the day when she will offer her body to her beloved in covenanted sexual love.

Spenser helps us to see that sexual passion tends toward generosity, loyalty, and risk-taking for the sake of others. No wonder, then, that it should so easily be taken up into love of neighbor. The result is the distinctive form of neighbor-love that I am calling true love—not because this is the only kind of love that is genuine, but because this term has a special resonance within the romantic tradition. What distinguishes true love from other forms of neighbor-love is that the lover gives himself or herself totally and exclusively to the other, often long before the commitment is solemnized in a public ceremony. True love is radical self-giving.

Radical Self-Giving

In a way, love of neighbor always involves self-giving. But in most instances it cannot and should not be as thorough-going as the self-giving that characterizes true love. In the daily round of life, we deal with all kinds of people, each of whom is of infinite worth and deserves our attention and care. Yet, precisely because we have obligations to a wide range of neighbors, we are forced to share our love as best we can. We can be totally present and available to anyone in need for a limited amount of time, but eventually our ongoing primary responsibilities kick in. No doubt the Good Samaritan had a wife to return to and children to feed. Even celibate priests, monks, and nuns, who minimize familial responsibilities in order to be available to everyone, go to great pains not to get too attached to or responsible for anyone in particular. Such attachments get in the way of wider availability. Only true love devotes itself to one person, holding nothing back. The covenanted life union of two persons covers every aspect of life. To be united in heart is to have a settled emotional attachment to each other. To be united in body is to be sexually related to each other, but also physically present to each other (living in the same place, sharing meals, sleeping in the same bed). To be united in mind is to be in conversation, engaged in the shared search for truth that is the signature of human social interaction. There are no lingering pockets of the single life, no built-in escape hatches. No separate checking accounts. No prenuptial agreements. No extramarital relationships. No friend or activity that is off-limits to either partner. I am well aware that there are couples who enter into unions with one or more such exceptions written into the contract. But such exceptions raise serious questions about the intention of the couple to give themselves wholly to each other.

I don't blame couples for hedging their bets. It is risky to give someone else a share in my body, my possessions, my emotional and intellectual life. Sometimes couples who are willing to go this route still hope that they can mitigate their risk by ensuring that each partner's gift of self occurs at the same time. The idea is that no one has to "go first." But this is mere fantasy. In real life, someone always goes first. In any case, true love demands that each lover give himself away to the beloved unilaterally—otherwise it is not a gift, but part of a negotiation. Traditional marriage rites reflect the unilateral character of the vows. Each party makes the vow while holding the other's right hand with his or her own. But after the first vows have been spoken, the couple looses hands so that the other party can deliberately take the other's hand before speaking his or her vows. In this way, both persons take the initiative in giving themselves away to the other.

In other words, there is no place for reciprocity in covenanted unions. To some extent, this is counterintuitive. I remember my Oklahoma grandmother always telling me that if someone loved me, I should love them back. That's probably not all that uncommon a thing for adults to say to children, and on the face of it, it seems like a reasonable thing to say. Certainly as adults we tend to think that if we offer love, it should be returned. But the problem is that "loving back" is not love, it is payback. True love does not seek payback, or a return on its investment, or even compensation for losses incurred. What each party to the union does, he or she does out of his or her own freedom. When I give myself in this way, I take on the risk of violation, betrayal, or indifference. There is no formula for safety here. I can give my heart to the gentlest and most trustworthy of people, but still I run the risk that my love will simply not be returned.

So is true love just a leap in the dark? Not if we are guided by the conventions of romantic literature. According to that tradition, to fall in love is to see the beloved as he or she is or could be. Falling in love is not about moving into darkness. It rises out of an insight into the beloved as a worthy recipient of the lover's gift of self. Nothing is expected in return.

This is not to say that the lover does not wish for anything. In the conventions of romantic love, the lover does not presume on being loved by the beloved. He wishes for his gift to be honored, and he hopes that his beloved has the same feelings for him—and that this is a movement of love having its birth in the beloved's own choice. In other words, true love seeks a genuine corresponding love, which may come about in response to the lover's initiative, or which may have long preceded it, but which possesses its own integrity, its own freedom, its own willingness to take on risk and suffer loss.

Self-Giving as a Way of Life

The notion of self-giving raises red flags for us these days, and so it should. In the name of self-giving, which translates into self-sacrifice, women have been told—and are still being told—to offer their lives as resources for the husbands they serve. In the name of self-giving, which can also be translated as self-exposure, victims of abuse can be told that acquiescing in their violation is a form of love. So I would like to remind everyone who is reading this book that each of us is of incalculable worth, created in the image of God. True lovers especially need to be reminded of this, because they are often at risk for having a low opinion of their worth. They are in the habit of not making much of themselves—which, for the most part, is not a bad habit to cultivate. As we have seen, true love emerges out of a vision of the beloved in all his or her beauty. If I think too highly of myself, it is all the more difficult to see my beloved clearly, and even more difficult to give my heart to her. I need to get myself out of the way, which in turn requires a measure of self-forgetfulness, the habit of thinking about others before thinking about myself. Unfortunately, humility often goes hand in hand with low self-esteem, which simply gets reinforced when one is confronted with a vision of the beloved in all his or her loveliness. This is not to say that those of us who are inclined to self-absorption and pride cannot fall in love. Of course we can. The sheer excellence of another may break through our self-love, just as the transfigured glory of Jesus broke through Peter's swaggering foolishness (Luke 9:28–36), and the voice of the risen Christ cut through Paul's blind arrogance (Acts 9:1–9). But the shock of discovering that I love someone of seemingly surpassing worth may do more than stop my pride in its tracks. It may cause me to feel as if I have no worth at all. This is why I want to state in the strongest possible terms that the self-giving associated with true love has nothing to do with self-abnegation or self-debasement. The worth of each of us lies ultimately in the fact that we belong to God. God's claim on us as God's creation defines our value—nothing else. Not even my own assessment of myself matters here. If we believe that God loves all of us—and I do—then each of us is infinitely worthy, because God's love is infinite. Nothing and no one can strip us of this worth, nor can we give it away. It is inalienable. Any relationship that invites us to deny our own worth and to degrade ourselves is not from God and has nothing to do with true love.

So if we want to get down to what self-giving really means in the dynamic of true love, we must understand how it is different from self-abasement. The assumption that self-giving is a form of self-abasement is fairly modern. It arises from the unbiblical assumption that the self's worth lies in its achievement of a certain measure of autonomy, the capacity to opt out of any relationship at a moment's notice. This is an essentially antisocial notion. It supposes that self-realization is a journey out of dependence on others into a condition in which one relies on oneself alone to define who one is. Such self-reliance then comes to be viewed as the quintessence of real freedom.

This modern idea is based in part on something that is true: maturity requires that we be able to keep our moral bearings in the face of social pressure. We must hold fast to our convictions even when the crowd or those in power urge otherwise. But maturity is not the same thing as self-reliance, and defining oneself over against the crowd is not the same thing as defining oneself over against the neighbor as such. When the German Lutheran pastor Dietrich Bonhoeffer stood almost alone in his refusal to cooperate with Hitler's attempt to turn German Protestantism into a wing of the Nazi movement, he relied first on God, and then on every shred of integrity he could grab hold of in the tattered Christian community. He did not turn away from community when he turned away from Hitler's regime. He turned all the more passionately *toward* any community that could strengthen his resolve and shore up his moral vision. For him, freedom and sanity lay in rejecting self-serving fellowships while embracing any fellowship committed to the love of neighbor. If anything, maturity and freedom lay in more dependence on God and the neighbor, not less.

Biblical Models of Self-Giving

Whenever the achievement of a fully-developed identity is equated with self-reliance, it becomes impossible to square self-worth with self-giving. If self-worth is associated with self-realization, it cannot also be associated with offering oneself in service to the neighbor. The self-worth that hinges on self-reliance is achieved by taking oneself back, reclaiming one's identity from the meddling hands of other people. But if our worth lies in God, then giving ourselves to God is not giving our worth away but returning to its source. And if, as the Bible seems to be saying in a thousand ways, submission to God's will means all kinds of self-giving to others, then giving ourselves in love to the beloved cannot involve a loss of worth. In fact, it should yield the opposite result, since self-giving is in accordance with God's will.

When all is said and done, giving ourselves away in love has nothing to do with losing worth or gaining it. So what *does* it have to do with? I've mentioned the Bible several times, so let's look at some biblical models. I am not going to restrict myself to models provided by the stories of sexual unions, because I think unions of heart and mind, if not of body, teach us important lessons—lessons that are all the more applicable to sexual unions, once bodily union is factored in. The three models I have chosen are Ruth and Naomi, Jacob and Rachel, and Jonathan and David.

Ruth and Naomi

Let's begin with the story of Ruth and Naomi (as found in the Book of Ruth). After Naomi's Moabite husband dies, leaving two sons who in turn die childless, Naomi resolves to return to her native Bethlehem, leaving her Moabite daughters-in-law behind. Ruth refuses to be parted from Naomi, and accompanies her into Israelite territory, where she eventually marries Boaz and becomes an ancestor of David. This story is famous for its witness to personal loyalty. But it can also be read as a story about self-giving for the sake of love. When Ruth accompanies Naomi to Bethlehem, she forfeits her original birthright. She does not lose her identity as a Moabite, but she forswears any advantage that this could bring her. Far from the protection of her birth family, she allows herself to become completely dependent on Naomi's circle of kin. As a foreigner, this move is fraught with risk, even danger.

Ruth's story highlights one of the costs frequently incurred by love. Love may require that we compromise or leave behind the identity and status we enjoy among our own family and people. This is certainly true for lovers who intend lifelong union. The union itself is uncharted territory, full of challenges to each partner's assumptions about who she is, what it means to be joined to someone else, how the living space should be arranged and maintained, how to raise children, and how to worship God, if at all. These are just a few of the areas where couples who have similar backgrounds and share the same cultural and ethnic identity are likely to discover chasms that separate them. But what about couples who come from different classes, different races, different religions? At least one of the lovers is going to feel like Ruth.

Thankfully, it's less common than it used to be for either the wife or the husband to adopt the other's social identity for the sake of unity. Households that span all kinds of social divides are on the increase, and that can only be a good thing. But in some ways this increases the challenge for each member of an interracial or inter-religious household. If I as a Christian were to marry a Muslim, and both of us retained our faith, it would not be enough for me simply to honor my partner's religion while keeping my distance from it. I would need to give myself over to as full, deep, and respectful a relationship with Islam as I enjoyed with my spouse. Human beings are not, after all, separable from the communities that shape them. I could not embrace my Muslim spouse without embracing Islam at the same time. This makes it seem as if I would have to become a Muslim myself, since we tend to assume that to embrace something is to become one with it. Not at all. In his excellent book *Exclusion and Embrace*, Miroslav Volf, a Croatian Baptist whose family suffered greatly at the hands of the Serbs in the early 1990s, reflects deeply on the dynamics of forgiveness and reconciliation. He concludes that when we embrace something, we open a space for it in our life and in our self-understanding. We neither absorb it nor do we intend to be absorbed by it, but we invite the connection that exists between it and us, along with the constant questions and irritations this may occasion, to become a dimension of our own identity.

Obviously, this kind of embrace, like the embrace that joins two differing partners together, inevitably brings change. I cannot engage in serious Christian-Muslim dialogue without my religious standpoint shifting in some way. It may shift in the direction of a stronger faith in Christ, but that doesn't mean that my Christianity hasn't been enriched and informed by my encounter with Islam. I could come up with a hundred other parallel examples. In each case the point would be the same. In every union there will be some kind of divide that calls each partner not only to embrace the partner in all his difference, but to *take in* that difference and to engage it fully. This may mean attending synagogue with a Jewish husband, or showing up at a political rally with a Republican wife. Whatever the case, we must struggle to maintain an openness to differences that are sure to challenge our identity and may well change it.

Jacob and Rachel

If Ruth's story is about giving up one's secure identity for love's sake, the story of Jacob and Rachel (Genesis 29–31) is about curtailing one's freedom. According to the account in Genesis, Jacob falls in love with his cousin Rachel, but her father, Laban, will not let Jacob marry her until Jacob serves him as a farmhand for seven years. When the seven years are up, Laban tricks Jacob by substituting Rachel's older sister, Leah, for Rachel on their marriage night. So Jacob works an additional seven years to gain his true love. In some ways this story, which relates so directly to sexual union, is harder to apply to our time than the story of Ruth and Naomi. But if we can get past the polygamy and the father's role in assigning his daughters in marriage, the story of Jacob highlights an important dimension of the self-giving involved in true love. Jacob does not give over his original identity to get Rachel, but he does give over his ability to do what he pleases. It is Laban, of course, who exacts this from Jacob. But the story's continuing power lies in the fact that, whether or not there is a wicked father-in-law around, and regardless of one's gender, union comes at the cost of freedom.

In Jacob's case this meant fourteen years of servitude. What might it mean today? Freedom is highly prized in our society. At the national level and in our public rhetoric, freedom generally means *political* freedom—being able to speak and vote one's mind. Since we are fortunate enough to enjoy considerable political freedom, our engagement with the issue of freedom at the personal level has more to do with our ability to make the best use of our political freedom. This is not true for everybody, of course. Racial minorities, gays and lesbians, undocumented workers—all these groups continue to deal with discrimination that narrows their range of choices. But for many people, freedom boils down to being able to make the best use of the choices life lays before us. The government may not get in the way of these choices, but other factors certainly do.

For instance, the size of my paycheck defines and delimits a whole range of options for me, from the space I live in to the medical care I have access to. Another major indicator of freedom is flexibility. In an extremely mobile society like ours, the amount of choice we have in pursuing a career is often directly linked to our ability to uproot ourselves at a moment's notice.

It is precisely here that couples find themselves most challenged. Single life offers a seemingly unlimited supply of flexibility. Not only can single people follow career opportunities wherever they may lead them, but they are sufficiently free of the obligation to support others that they can leave lucrative positions to pursue vocations that can't support a family. When I was single, I could imagine serving as a priest anywhere. I would like to think that this is still the case, but for all practical purposes, it is not. I have obligations as a husband and father that make me less flexible—which means less free—than I was twenty-some years ago. So it is for anyone in a committed union. Whenever a vocational or career opportunity arises, each party is bound to assess the consequences for his partner and for the household as a whole. What effect will a move or a salary cut have on the other's job, the other's family, and the children they are raising together? Or, to turn it around, how willing is the partner to leave a job he likes in order to support his beloved in a new venture?

These are unavoidable questions for most couples, and there are no easy answers. It is important that couples preparing to enter into a lifelong covenant talk together about how they might adjudicate decisions that require one of them to give up something. My own view is that the self-giving inherent in true love demands that both partners be willing, if necessary, to forego their options. It is even better if they can approach the loss of freedom as a common problem, willingly taken on by each and creatively addressed by both together. In the final analysis, true love—if it is true—trumps career and any other attachment, whether to place or lifestyle.

Jonathan and David

Now we come to Jonathan and David (1 Samuel 18–20), whose story also raises the question of career, but presses it a little further. To put it in the starkest terms, if Jacob gave up his freedom for Rachel, Jonathan, by siding with David against Jonathan's father, Saul, gave up his future for David. There are some indications that the relationship of David and Jonathan may have been sexual. For

instance, Saul expresses contempt for Jonathan's love of David
(1 Samuel 20:30), and David, lamenting his friend's death, says
that his love surpassed that of women (2 Samuel 1:26). However
we understand it, this was a relationship that transcended familial and political loyalties and goals. In the end, David benefited
from the relationship far more than Jonathan, though when he
entered into power, he honored Jonathan's family, so it seems that
David was sincere in his love of Jonathan. There can be no question about Jonathan, however. He gave up everything for David:
first, the trust of his father, and, ultimately, the kingdom that he
would have inherited had not David withdrawn his support of
Saul's campaigns against the Philistines. How does this relate to
us today?

The epic scale of the biblical narrative need not keep us from
applying this story to ourselves. Jonathan gave up his future as King
of Israel for the sake of David. Self-giving for one's beloved may
well mean letting a career falter or die. Is this right? Who should
decide which career will prosper, if it is a choice between one or
the other? These are difficult questions. In our own day, we make
every effort to make both careers possible. But what if there is no
choice? What if one partner is offered a professorship in New York
City, and the other partner is offered a senior position in a presti-
gious law practice in San Francisco? Some couples might choose
to live apart at this point, so that both careers can be pursued. But
this may well be the preamble to breakup. What can hold a couple
together under these circumstances? Only the willingness of both
partners to forego promotion for the sake of the union. In the past,
the burden has fallen on women in the professions to yield to their
husbands' career needs. This is unacceptable, of course. Each partner must be equally willing to let everything go for the sake of the
other. The ultimate decision should be guided by a consideration
of what is best for the union.

These three stories illustrate three ways in which the offering
of one's life to another plays out: Ruth gives away her past; Jacob

gives away his present; Jonathan gives away his future. Although not all of these stories is about a sexual union, each demonstrates an essential aspect of the gift of self on which a lifelong covenanted union depends. This gift, freely given, is the very material out of which the union is made. It is to sacred union what water is to baptism and bread and wine are to communion—the outward and visible sign of the true love that animates a union and constitutes its holiness.

The Self-Giving of Jesus

For Christians, of course, the paradigm for all self-giving is Jesus Christ, whose entire work is summed up by Paul as a self-emptying. I would like to conclude this chapter by briefly considering Paul's words as they relate to the subject of true love:

> Be disposed among yourselves as Christ Jesus was, who,
> though in the form of God did not consider equality with
> God a thing to be grasped, but emptied himself, taking the
> form of a slave, being born in the likeness of human beings.
> And being found in human shape, he humbled himself
> and became obedient as far as death, even the death of the
> cross. (Philippians 2:5–8, my translation)

On the face of it, this passage is obviously relevant to the whole topic of self-giving—indeed, no exploration of true love from a Christian perspective could avoid looking at it—but it also presents us with a problem. Paul's hymn to Jesus' outpouring of himself can easily be read by analogy to the dynamics of true love.

Paul portrays Jesus as a lover who unilaterally gives over his past, his present, and his future for the sake of his beloved, who in this case is the entire human race. He voluntarily leaves behind his identity as one who is equal to God. In doing so, he gives up his freedom and becomes a slave. Finally, he even accepts death on the cross. From the perspective of Good Friday (though not of Easter), Jesus gives up any future he or his disciples might have hoped for. Looked at in this way, this passage seems to identify self-giving with a loss of self-worth—the very thing I warned against earlier. Jesus lays his glory to one side to endure the indignity of slavery, and worse yet for my argument, his self-abnegation exposes him to cruel treatment at the hands of his beloved. Is Christian romanticism an invitation to abuse, after all?

It would be, if this were the correct reading of the passage. We are right to say that Philippians 2:5–8 provides us with the proper context for understanding true love from a Gospel point of view, inasmuch as it clearly presents Jesus as a lover of the human race, unilaterally placing himself in his beloved's hands. But we will misinterpret the passage if we read it only as a portrait of Jesus' relationship to his beloved. It is as much or more a portrait of his relationship to the Father, at whose bidding he set out on his mission of love in the first place. Jesus' descent into slavery may be unilateral as far as his relationship with humankind goes, but it is not unilateral with respect to the Father. Jesus is clearly responding to a command, as becomes evident in verses 9–11, in which Paul describes how the Father rewards him for his work—and in so doing glorifies himself as the one who commissioned it. Thus Jesus' enslavement is best understood not as his subjection to his beloved but as the manifestation of his subjection to the Father, to whom he had been equal but whom he now serves in his capacity as Son of Man. Such a reading is consistent with Paul's seeming suggestion that the "form of a slave" is the same thing as "human shape" and "the likeness of human beings." To be human is to be God's slave, but for Paul this is not a bad thing. In Romans 6:22 Paul writes: "Now that you have been freed from sin and have become slaves of God, the return you get is sanctification." So by doing God's will humbly and without complaint, Jesus reveals himself to be not only truly human but an exemplary human. At the same time, God's will turns out to be nothing other than the redemption and sanctification of the human race through the ministry of Jesus, who is both lover and neighbor, both servant of God and servant of humankind on God's behalf. Finally, on this reading, Jesus' self-emptying is shown *not* to entail a loss of self-worth. Quite the opposite. To be God's slave (rather than the slave of sin, or, for that matter, the slave of any human being) is itself the perfection and glory of human nature. As Paul puts it elsewhere: "Now that you have been freed from sin and enslaved to God, the advantage you get is sanctification" (Romans 6:22).

The correctness of this reading is borne out by what immediately follows. Continuing to urge the Philippian Christians to serve one another in love, Paul writes: "For it is God who is at work in you, enabling you both to will and to work for his good pleasure" (2:13). Paul is asking the Philippians to imitate Christ's obedience to the Father by placing the interests of others higher than their own (2:4). This section closes with Paul saying, "Even if I am being poured out as a libation over the sacrifice and offering of your faith, I am glad and rejoice with all of you" (2:17). The important thing to note here is that, for Paul, assuming the form of a servant is a cause for rejoicing. He has long since left privilege behind, but the worth he possesses, as someone called and loved by God, is unassailable.

I am spending time with this passage because, read rightly, it has a direct bearing on Christian romanticism, and might be regarded as its manifesto. Once again I am reminded of the reversal the troubadours effected on the classic Christian identification of Christ as groom and the soul as bride. Philippians certainly shows us a Christ who sets out as husband to win back his spouse at any cost to himself. But because Paul invites us to regard Christ's self-emptying as exemplary, he anticipates the romantic identification of the lover—regardless of gender—with Christ. This is why it is fitting that the solemn blessing of a marriage in the Book of Common Prayer (BCP) begins by offering thanks for God's "tender love in sending Jesus Christ to come among us, to be born of a human mother, and to make the way of the cross to be the way of life" (BCP 430). Authentic romance is nothing less than the imitation of Christ, and the true lover is nothing other than a disciple who, whether she knows it or not, is walking on the way of the cross. If we keep this in mind, we will not be misled into thinking that we are ultimately in service to our beloved. It is God who enables our love in the first place. It is God who breaks through the fog of selfishness and reveals the beloved to us in all his or her potential glory. And it is with the vision of God, in the company of our beloved and of countless others, that we shall be rewarded at journey's end.

1. Do you and your partner come from similar religious, social, and economic backgrounds? How do you address and deal with any differences? How do you want your life together to be the same as or different from the way each of you grew up?

2. Are children in your future? Do you want to raise them in a religious tradition? Which one? How large a role do you want the Church to play in your child's life?

3. How do we learn the humility that is not self-deprecation? How can I practice true humility with my partner? With my neighbor? With God?

Exercise:

Separately, each of you write out your ideal job—the position you dream of having. Be as detailed as you are able. Come back together and share what you've written with your partner. Now imagine that each of you has been offered this exact job, but in cities that are hundreds of miles apart. What will you do?

FOUR

The Discipline of Fidelity

ROMANTICISM TENDS TO LOCATE THE BEGINNING OF TRUE love in a single event. But it doesn't usually happen that way. The awakening of sexual desire, the rush of insight into the other's sheer otherness, the decision to give one's heart to the other—these are the three basic movements that constitute falling in love. But they seldom occur all at once, and they don't necessarily happen in that order. It is like coming to belief. When we talk about our own faith journey, we may well focus on a single moment of conversion. But we know that many seemingly minor events led up to it, and that a long and sometimes painful process of integration followed it. So it is with the maturation of true love.

The process of living into our love may be looked at as the working out of the implications of this love for our lives, as well as the mastering of the virtues or disciplines required to transform an initial commitment into a lifelong reality. For example, when sexual desire coincides with an acute awareness of the other as neighbor, so that the lover yields his heart to the beloved, it is safe to say that in that moment the lover's sexual desire is shaped and directed by the intention of faithfulness. But faithfulness is not the automatic and instant byproduct of falling in love, any more than true love is its immediate achievement. Faithfulness is a habit of mind and a discipline of the will that requires attention and practice over time. In this chapter I will explore what practicing faithfulness entails.

Sexual Fidelity

Let's begin, then, by reflecting on the discipline of faithfulness, or (to be very clear) sexual fidelity. The word *fidelity* is taken directly from the Latin *fidelitas,* which in turn is built on *fides,* meaning "faith" or "trust." It does not refer to having faith, but to being worthy of the faith that someone else has in you. This is why I think that the intention of being faithful is automatically a part of falling in love. Keep in mind that true love is not reducible to sexual desire, but infuses this desire with genuine respect and a longing to be joined in earthly union to this person and to no other. A merely sexual relationship can suddenly be transformed into one of true love, and then the couple is traversing new ground. The sexual act may be the same, but its content is not. The lover who has given her heart to the beloved approaches sex not only as a supplicant (any clever seducer can do that), but also with the genuine hope of permanent union. She wants her beloved to think well of her—to be regarded as someone who can be counted on as steady and un-wavering in her love. In short, she wants to be seen as true, and to be proven over time to be such.

There is little room for self-doubt about this in the first flush of true love. As the romantic tradition would put it, falling in love is total capitulation. The lover who has given herself over to the be-loved can no more imagine herself being unfaithful than she can imagine not being in love. From this perspective, fidelity is not a dis-cipline at all. It is an essential ingredient of the lover's happiness. In the object of her love she finds the true direction and fulfillment of her life: How could she head off in another direction without doing herself in? Literature and drama offer many examples of women and men whose steadfastness in love seems to well up from deep inside themselves. One character whose story continues to stay with me is Forrest Gump, from the movie of that name. In spite of his mental deficiencies, he is a model of fidelity in difficult circumstances, re-maining faithful to his love throughout his life.

Nevertheless, for most of us, even while we are completely given over to faithfulness as a crucial component of our own happiness, sexual fidelity encounters us right from the beginning as a demand addressed to us from outside of ourselves. The beloved requires it. Why? Because she is giving us the gift of herself, and is not willing that it be squandered. It can be very irritating to be asked to do something that we were intending to do anyway, as if we needed to be told. But this situation strikes me as not being like that. The beloved requires fidelity of me, and I (if I am honest) require it of my beloved, despite the fact that each of us is perfectly aware that the other wants to be faithful on his or her own. I *require* the fidelity of my partner (as distinct from simply taking it for granted), because my own sense of myself as worthy of being loved depends on it.

Here we come down to bedrock. Worth is deeper than love, and comes before it, because it is love's wellspring. This is why giving oneself to another in love cannot include the surrender of one's worth, since that is what motivates the gift and what constitutes its value. Inherent in the inalienable dignity of the lover is the fact that the gift of love confirms our individuality; it neither compromises it nor calls it into question.

Because of the wholehearted self-giving inherent in true love, it is easy to misinterpret this self-giving as a submergence of oneself in the other, tantamount to a loss of self. But the requirement of fidelity clearly demonstrates that selfhood itself can never be given away. Autonomy can be relinquished in the name of service, but the dignity of one's identity as a child of God, and, I would add, the freedom that enables us to love or not to love—these cannot be given away. True love may look like two people becoming one, but it is not. True love derives its spiritual beauty from the fact that two people are really giving themselves to each other. It is an exchange, not a fusion.

In the original conclusion of Book 3 of *The Faerie Queene* (right after Britomart rescues Amoret from Busirane), Spenser describes the ecstatic reunion of the two largely allegorical figures,

Scudamour and Amoret, as their virtual submergence in each other to form a single whole, a hermaphrodite. In the second edition, which offered Books 4 to 6 in addition to the original three, Spenser changes the ending: the reunion is postponed. Since Spenser still has use for Scudamour and Amoret as independent characters—they both show up in Book 4, still looking for each other—it is obvious that Spenser changed the ending so that he would still have both characters to work with. But was this the only reason? Had he lived to finish his epic, would Spenser have described their eventual reunion differently? I suspect so, because, as the epic progresses, both characters seem more like real people and less like allegorical figures—which is my point: real lovers are not two halves of a whole. Each is an irreducible whole, a child of God headed for the reign of God.

This is why I dislike "unity candles" at weddings. The union we refer to when we speak of sacred unions is not the obliteration of the space that separates the lover from the beloved, the formation of one composite person where there were two. It is the creation of a new community united in love, but made up of two distinct persons engaged in neighborly service to each other. Needless to say, most couples are surprised (and perhaps dismayed) when I ask them to reconsider their decision to include a unity candle in the ceremony—or at least to reflect on it as a decision, and not something mandated by popular custom. (I do consider it their decision, having long ago given up the false notion that it is worth ruining a couple's wedding over something I can certainly live with if I have to.) Increasingly, couples are allowing the candle to take on a different meaning by inviting their parents to light it. When this happens, the candle immediately becomes the symbol for the joining of two families rather than two people. I am far more comfortable with this approach, since it would never occur to anyone to think that two families become one in such a way as to lose their separate identities. In any case, most couples who think it over decide either to have their parents light the unity candle or to do away with it entirely. They are helped in this direction when I tell them that, immediately following the exchange of vows and the exchange of the rings, I wrap my stole around their joined hands as I say, "What God has joined together, let no one put asunder." This literal "tying of the knot" speaks, I think, to what most couples really think they are doing when they commit themselves to each other. Union understood as binding is quite different from union understood as fusion. Two stalks of wheat tied together to form a sheaf are still two stalks. What's more, the union resulting from the profession of life vows is not something the couple effect all by themselves. It requires the encircling love and expectation of the gathered community and, above all, God's love and grace, wrapping them close.

All of which is to say, personal integrity is essential to the viability of a union. I do not say autonomy, which has little to do with personal integrity. Autonomy means being in charge of one's life, and this is something we give up when we enter into lifelong union. In true love I give everything away to the beloved—my heart, my body, and my autonomy; everything except my soul, by which I mean my identity as someone made in the image of God, and ultimately accountable to God alone. This nobility is not itself the gift; it is what underwrites the gift.

The requirement of fidelity is the flip side of this gift. Fidelity is not simply abstention from sex with other persons. It is a positive regard for the dignity of the partner and an attitude of thanks for the partner's self-offering. My beloved requires it of me, and I require it of my beloved. How is this requirement to be fulfilled? As I suggested earlier, this is not a meaningful question for true love in its early days. Both partners want to be faithful, and fully intend to be. But intention by itself is not enough. We really are creatures of habit. This does not mean that we can't kick habits we don't want, or that we can't be transported into entirely new behavioral territory through cataclysms like religious conversion or falling in love. But new lives require new habits. A newcomer to religious faith may be full of fervor, but may still have trouble remembering to give thanks to God before eating, or not to take God's name in vain. These may seem like small things, but attention to them helps build the spiritual muscle that will be needed when one's faith comes under fire. So it is with true love: there are daily disciplines that can both affirm that love and anchor it securely.

The Discipline of Fidelity

Flirting

First of all, we can learn to communicate our nonavailability clearly and unambiguously. This is easier said than done. No matter how committed we are, there are few of us who don't derive some satisfaction from the sexual attention of others. That's not a bad thing in itself. But if the attention is expressly invited, or we don't take sufficient care to avoid the appearance of making such an invitation, then there is a problem.

Sexual fidelity requires abstention not only from sex with others but also from flirtation, and the avoidance of situations that invite temptation or communicate willingness to cross boundaries. This is as much a question of respecting everyone who is around you as well as respecting the rights of your partner. I liken this to the rules of the workplace. The level of professionalism that we expect from one another includes careful attention to personal boundaries. The promise to be faithful is a public promise because it pertains to anyone with whom one might otherwise have been involved. When I say "I will not be sexually involved with anyone but you," I'm saying that the boundary separating my body from everybody but my partner is as unambiguous and nonnegotiable in a nightclub as in the office, on the subway as in the classroom.

Fantasies

The discipline of fidelity also requires that we not intentionally fantasize about sex outside of the union. This is not just a matter of keeping our thoughts clean and our intentions pure. Imaginary infidelity does real damage to the partner who engages in it, because it constitutes a kind of unfaithfulness to oneself. Our own sense of well-being and self-worth depends greatly on our sense of being at one with ourselves. If we are single-minded and single-hearted, if we know our own mind and are certain about the direction we are headed, then we can face all kinds of external problems with a measure of calm. But if we are at loggerheads with ourselves, no matter how much we may seem to be in control of our piece of the world, we will have no peace.

The Letter of James (1:8) warns us not to be "double-minded," wavering constantly between faith and doubt. James is not referring to the critical edge that must be part of any faith that is searching and self-aware. He is talking about the kind of willful distractedness that allows things and people other than God to become the objects of worship. The result of this is an inner turmoil that is self-inflicted. So it is with fidelity. To toy with imaginary infidelities is only to risk tearing one's own heart in two.

The internet has opened up a whole new medium for communication that can be particularly tricky in this regard. It is easy to think of websites and even e-mail conversations as impersonal, because they can seem to be so completely sealed off from the rest of one's life. But even if they are sealed off—which they can never really be—they are certainly personal, even if they remain one-sided. They are personal because in our own person, we are taking the affection we owe to our partner and propelling it elsewhere.

Availability to Each Other

Not all the disciplines of fidelity are restrictive. The other side of abstention from sex with all others is total availability to one's partner. This doesn't just happen—it has to be worked on. We all know that various pressing obligations—making a living, being parents, pursuing vocations—can distract partners from each other.

Also, sheer familiarity may dull our sense of the other's splendor and mystery. Finally, the aging process itself can cause partners to drift apart sexually. All these problems arise, it seems to me, from a failure to pay sufficient attention to each other. I don't just mean sexual attention here, although that is important. I mean being acutely aware of and interested in what is really going on in one's partner's life and heart. This takes setting aside time every day to check in, to ask questions, to listen, to be in physical and emotional touch with each other. Such attention is not the same thing as the invasion of privacy, or chumminess. It should be just the opposite: an occasion to honor the space that opens up between partners when they rediscover each other as neighbors.

This is more like the attention that we give to God when we set aside time each day for prayer. When we pray, we renew the covenant that binds us to God in faith. When two partners exercise the discipline of attention, they also renew their covenant with each other, in the context of the changing circumstances of their lives. True love is the conjunction of sexual desire and love of neighbor. But over time it may be better described as an intimacy constantly fed and deepened by greater and greater appreciation of one's partner as a fellow pilgrim—a pilgrim on a path that sometimes includes the partner directly, and sometimes just needs the partner to stand by as a completely trustworthy supporter. If sexual fidelity is the honoring of the beloved's inalienable worth as an individual, fidelity is best strengthened by going to the trouble of keeping that worth in full view.

However, the discipline of attention may seem to raise problems of its own. How much should I attend to my partner to the exclusion of other people? In a way this question is based on a false premise. As we saw in the last chapter, true love never excludes God or the neighbor, because true love catches us up into a larger dynamic that has universal fellowship as its goal. Yet we don't have to consider the rationale for sexual fidelity very long without realizing that fidelity has to do with more than sex. It sums up the total availability owed by the lover to the beloved in acknowledgment of the beloved's gift of self. So how do we reconcile fidelity with the broader implications of neighbor-love?

Nonexclusive Exclusivity

Let's go back to the original assertion that true love never excludes God or other neighbors. If that is the case, then the demand of fidelity should not be construed as prohibiting companionship and affection for other people besides one's partner. We can and should show concern for the well-being of our neighbors and a genuine desire to serve and care for them. In a previous paragraph I compared attention to one's partner to time devoted to prayer. But the analogy goes beyond the discipline of attention. It is impossible to pray for any length of time without being lifted by the Spirit of God into the presence of the neighbor. In just the same way, true love does not close us off from humanity; it thrusts us more deeply into its midst. Fidelity must ultimately support this outward reach. I think it does so in several ways.

First, the requirement of fidelity is a constant reminder of what is owed to the beloved. What is owed is no less than an acknowledgment that the beloved's gift of self is something of surpassing worth. Fidelity is that acknowledgment. (Note that I am not equating fidelity with self-giving here. Fidelity is a discipline taken up in recognition of my partner's claim on me, which I am bound to recognize and honor if I have accepted my partner's gift of self, *even if I have not really given myself in return.*)

Second, by keeping my focus on my partner rather than on other competitors for my attention, sexual and otherwise, fidelity schools me in neighbor-love. This is not as paradoxical as it sounds. When fidelity acknowledges the surpassing worth of the beloved, it recognizes that the beloved's worth is independent of her evaluation by her partner. This is the same thing as recognizing the beloved as the neighbor, whose otherness (in this case, whose surpassing worthiness) can never be annexed or obliterated by a faithless partner. The discipline of fidelity teaches the one who practices it about the essential otherness of the neighbor. There can be no greater spiritual practice than this, because it trains us in the fundamental principle of God's reign: willingness to be identified with others who are completely different from ourselves.

Third, fidelity, as a practice and discipline shared by both partners, bears fruit in a union of two people who share a common experience of and commitment to love of neighbor. The respect and space they have learned to afford each other, together with the attention and care they are in the habit of giving each other, will inevitably sensitize them to the neighbor who calls to them, not as individuals, but as a couple. More accurately, the more work they do to honor each other by being faithful sexually and in every other way, the more they will be ready to experience the claim of the neighbor as something that is addressed to them together, and the more they will be able, as a couple, to respond to that claim. In this respect sacred unions have a lot in common with monastic communities.

At first glance, these two states of life seem radically different, since unions are sexual relationships, and monks and nuns are celibate. But if we reflect a little we will see that these two ways of life share the same purpose: learning how to love the neighbor—and the same strategy: practicing this virtue on a select few. For monastics, the "select few" comprises the brothers or sisters with whom one shares a rule and a house. For partners in a union, the "few" is one. In both cases, the unity achieved within the primary community is meant to bear fruit in a united witness to the world.

So fidelity moves from an exclusive focus on one's partner to the development of a partnership that is increasingly outward-facing. We should note, however, that it does not always feel or look like that along the way. Outside observers may find it hard to see the distinction between intense attention directed by true lovers toward each other, and collective self-absorption. Friends and family may find it hard not to experience the establishment of a lifelong union as a diminishment of their claim on either party or both.

A parent may subtly suggest that it would be nice to have some "family time" before the wedding without your fiancé there. An old friend stops returning e-mails because, as it turns out, she does not want to "intrude" in the relationship. I don't want to exaggerate this point, but I don't want to discount it, either. For the most part, the friends and families of both parties are a tremendous source of support for a couple, since they have an investment in their happiness. But this investment can go hand in hand with behavior that subverts the couple's relationship at every turn.

This should come as no surprise. It is human nature to rejoice in the happiness of others; it is also human nature to oppose any new configuration of relationships that seems to leave us out in the cold. The highest compliment John's Gospel pays John the Baptist is to show how he resists this temptation. According to this Gospel, when John the Baptist's disciples come to him complaining that the crowds are choosing to be baptized by Jesus rather than by John, this is his reply: "He who has the bride is the bridegroom. The friend of the bridegroom, who stands and hears him, rejoices greatly at the bridegroom's voice. For this reason my joy has been fulfilled. He must increase, but I must decrease" (John 3:29–30). The point of the evangelist's compliment is that it is unusual to encounter generosity where jealousy might have been expected.

Challenges to Fidelity from Unexpected Quarters

When we *do* meet up with jealousy within our community of support, it is often difficult to recognize it for what it is, because it comes disguised in many forms: veiled (or not so veiled) warnings about one's intended partner, requests for private time to talk through a personal problem, inappropriate investment in decisions surrounding the forthcoming ceremony. Such behavior may be perplexing, and when it becomes clear what is going on, it can be painful.

It may also present a challenge to the fidelity of either partner, whether we are talking about sexual fidelity or fidelity in the broader sense of attention. The period of engagement and the first year of covenanted partnership can be a complicated and uncomfortable time for a couple as they focus primarily on their relationship, while simultaneously trying to assure loved ones that they are not abandoning them. The temptation here is for one or both of the parties to allow their primary focus on each other to be blurred. Over time, a couple learns how to balance the claims of friends and family against the claim of the union, but the time of greatest tension is the time of greatest vulnerability, when each partner is struggling with the anxiety and uncertainty of transition. Sometimes the joy we feel in discovering our true love masks the loss we are also experiencing, or we are well aware of our grief but are ashamed of it. It may be hard to admit that I long for the familiarity of my old apartment, or that I resent not being able to withdraw into privacy whenever it suits me, or that I miss the attentions of others interested in my "eligibility" as a single person.

One of the challenges of the early days is to recognize and accept the fact that loss is an inevitable component of the journey into union. But the challenge is also to be faithful to one's partner, even in those terrible moments when union seems to come at too high a cost. This is where it may prove especially helpful to remember that fidelity is not a feeling but an obligation. If you feel like bolting, you may well get little encouragement from your old support team to stick it out. What will get you through is sheer dogged faithfulness, the refusal to turn your gaze away from your partner or to seek comfort from any other source than your partner. It is such faithfulness, born of duty and stubbornness, that forges unions able to be truly present to family, to friends, and to the world.

1. What does fidelity mean to you in the specific context of your relationship?

2. Do you experience faithfulness to each other in your relationship as a window to the world, through which you love and care for your neighbors? Or is it a door that shuts out the world? Which do you want it to be, and how will you achieve that?

3. Do you know deep inside that you trust your partner to be faithful? If so, why do you trust your partner? If not, why not?

Exercise:

Begin with each of you naming something from your world that tests your commitment to fidelity. How do you deal with this temptation or challenge within yourself? Now that your partner knows about it, how do you hope he or she will deal with it? Use this as an opportunity to establish a way you can deal together with the inevitable troubles that will stretch your commitment.

The second part of this exercise is done by each partner alone. Find a quiet place and search within yourself for something that you would not share with your partner. There will always be things in your life that are not beneficial to share. Name that for yourself, and examine why you choose not to share it. What are your reasons for not wanting to share this with your partner? Be clear with yourself about these reasons. Do they have to do with not wanting to cause your partner pain, or are you just protecting yourself from fully engaging your relationship with your partner?

FIVE

The Household

THE POSSIBILITY OF A UNION ARISES WHEN TWO PEOPLE fall in love with each other, both having freely taken the initiative (explicitly or implicitly) to offer themselves fully to the other in heart, body, and mind. When that offer is accepted by each party, and the claim and dignity of the giver is honored by the receiver's vow of fidelity, the union comes into being. But the union finds outward and visible expression in the creation of a home, through the combination of traditions, values, and patterns of exchange that constitute the union as a household. How do we get from love to householding—that is, to the particular give-and-take, the culture, the stories that make up the distinctive signature of a union?

Building a Household

A household is a community of two or more people living under the same roof. There are all kinds of households that are not grounded in a sexual union. Some are relatively casual, like four or five undergraduate students sharing a suite in a residential hall. Others are as committed as any marriage, like convents or monastic houses. All groups of people living together develop rules, traditions, and patterns of interaction that ensure a measure of predictability, order, and fairness in their common life. At the casual end of the spectrum, this may be no more than a schedule ensuring that everyone does a fair share of the cleaning. But when lifelong commitment is factored in, the stakes are much higher.

For a group of monks or nuns, it matters very much that there be a rule that governs every aspect of life, so that the disagreements that arise in everyday situations can be resolved efficiently and fairly. For a couple entering into lifelong union, it is essential that there be sufficient agreement about their common life so that they are able, as the Book of Common Prayer puts it, to "be a sign of God's reconciling love in a broken and sinful world." Here, too, the construction of a viable household requires some kind of agreed-upon set of expectations and rules.

Explicitly or implicitly, we have already considered the rules that any couple must agree to and take to heart if the union is going to last. Sexual fidelity is absolutely crucial, followed closely by the duty to be a real companion to one's partner. It is also essential that the union bear fruit in service to others. But households are not built out of principles alone. They are built out of the application of those principles to everyday life. Unlike monastic communities, couples cannot rely on a written set of rules, such as the Benedictine Rule, to live by. And, since every household is unique, they cannot appeal to any one school of thought that will guide them as they feel their way toward an understanding of their own unique identity as a household.

There is no formula for success. All kinds of competing obligations need to be identified and balanced; traditions and values inherited from the partners' families of origin must be honored and weighed; the new spiritual terrain that rises before them like an uncharted world must be explored and mapped.

Some couples make their way through these decisions by way of a series of negotiations and compromises. But it is more in the spirit of true love for both parties to assume that whatever results from the coming together of their two journeys will be a surprise to both of them. The dynamics of householding, like the dynamics of true love, depend on acts of generosity, not on wheeling and dealing. Building a life together is not a business transaction. I am not saying that working out the details of life together does not involve some trade-offs ("We can have a dog if you promise to do half the walking"), but the decisions that build up the union are born of generosity and patience, and they typically involve a unilateral concession or bestowal by one of the partners, with no expectation or desire to be "paid back."

Let's say I like background music at meals, and you find that fundamentally irritating. So I learn to do without a CD at dinner, because I really want you to have what you want. I may even end up joining you in your preference. Or let's say I don't like shoes being worn in the apartment. You think that is fussy and overweening, but for my sake you remove your shoes every time you come through the front door, without complaint or comment. Again, I might revise my eating habits to accommodate a vegetarian partner, rise earlier or later in order to dovetail with my partner's schedule, or modify my spending patterns out of respect for my partner's values. In any case, the creation of a household is something that we achieve, step by step. Each step is a sort of recapturing of our initial experience of falling in love, in which we let our self-giving find concrete expression in ordinary acts.

When Disagreements Arise

This is painstaking work from which no couple is exempt, but such sacrifices, made ungrudgingly as acts of love, are the very fabric of any healthy union. They give it its strength and its resilience under pressure. Negotiated settlements often have the opposite effect. They lodge in the lining of the household like foreign substances, reminders of the times we have behaved like competitors rather than lovers. Once a couple has identified a major area of disagreement, and it becomes apparent that this disagreement is not going to become an occasion for self-giving on either side, it is vital that the couple not resort to bargaining ("I agree to forego having children, but then my career must take priority when we are deciding where to move"). It would be better to break off the relationship than to do that, because such agreements will always yield distance if not divorce.

Religion is the one area in which substantial and persistent difference does not seem to pose a threat to a household's unity. Perhaps this is because reverence for and curiosity about other faiths is itself a dimension of religious faith. Thus, we can retain our own religious convictions and still affirm faith journeys that are different from our own, and we can do this without the slightest compromise. But even here, it is important that a couple take its differences seriously. In the spirit of interfaith dialogue, both partners should actively discuss and explore each other's faith and, where it is possible and appropriate, they should attend worship services and religious ceremonies together. Deciding how to raise children in an interfaith household presents more of a challenge.

Children benefit greatly by being raised in a religious tradition and within a worshipping faith community, and there is no reason that the children of an interfaith couple shouldn't grow up in two communities at once. If this is possible, I would strongly urge it. But sometimes a commitment to one faith or the other has to be made on the child's behalf. For instance, one side or both may call for formal incorporation of an infant into its fellowship, such as male circumcision or infant baptism. There is no reason that this should stand in the way of raising the child with exposure to both religions, but it does force the parents to decide which religion will take priority. This is another decision that should not be negotiated. If I am counseling an interfaith couple that expects to be raising children at some point, I strongly encourage them to begin struggling with this question right away, and not to wait until they are under pressure to decide quickly. This may be for each of them an occasion for a profound and spiritually productive act of self-giving.

The Mission of Union

As partners move through this process of forming a household, it may help them to frame and focus their decisions if they recognize that they are actually engaged in founding an institution—something with an identity and a direction that may well outlive them. I will go a step further and say that when a couple sets up house, they are transforming themselves into a corporation that, like any corporation, exists to pursue a range of goals. I don't want to be misunderstood here. The corporations we often hear about these days are national and transnational entities whose chief mission is to make a profit. But the not-for-profit world is also full of corporations, and most religious congregations and monastic houses are corporations as well. For any group or enterprise to be incorporated simply means that it is able to operate collectively as a legally recognized agent. But legal recognition does not get at the essence of what it means to be a corporation, since the real question is what it is that is being recognized when incorporation occurs. Clearly, what is being recognized is the existence of a group of people with a stated mission, who have so organized themselves as to ensure the perpetuation of that mission by their successors. Such a group can exist whether it is recognized by the state or not, as any religious minority banned by a hostile government will tell you. So when I compare a household to a corporation, I am not thinking about profit or power or even legal recognition (in many places same-sex unions are not legally recognized, let alone the households they establish). I am thinking about the establishment of life goals that not only reflect the couple's common vision, but reflect as well their witness to anyone who joins them on life's journey, be they children, close friends, permanent guests, or fellow travelers. These goals certainly include mutual joy and the benefit of shared resources; they may include raising children; one hopes they will include hospitality and service to the larger community. My point is that, like any corporation, each household has its own culture, its own formal and informal rules, its own criteria for measuring success. So if we want to assess the health and character of a household, it makes sense to determine what its mission is, to evaluate the mission, and to see what bearing it has on how the household actually functions. This forces us to ask hard questions about money, stewardship, time-management, and how much cost we are willing bear for the sake of our professed moral and religious commitments.

Having gone out of my way to be clear that corporations do not necessarily have anything to do with business, I must admit that the notion of the household as a corporation was first suggested to me by a friend (I'll call him Bill) who works in the business world. At first this made me reluctant to apply his insights to householding, lest the dynamics of life together in a committed relationship be reduced to the selfish give-and-take of commerce. But over time I have come to see that this is not what Bill has in mind—he regards his family as the polar opposite of his life in business. When he identifies disciplines and strategies within the world of business that apply to successful householding, he sees these as disciplines and strategies that pre-exist free enterprise and transcend it. In any case, Bill would say that the success of a family depends on its founders (the adult partners) being absolutely clear about its mission. Once the household mission is clear, everything else follows. Since Bill is a financial consultant, it is no surprise that for him the first priority is to decide where the household income is going to be directed, and why. But he is equally clear about how and with whom he spends his time, why his children go to school where they do, why he votes the way he does, and how all these decisions are made (he and his wife decide everything together). What I find challenging here is the notion that a household is not something haphazard—precisely because the union that stands at the heart of it is meant to be lifelong, it calls for some planning. I find that I myself resist too much of an emphasis on planning. Ultimately, the future is in God's hands, and there is a limit to how much we can try to second-guess that future without getting into spiritual trouble. Bill is not trying to exert total control over his life—he is simply trying to be a responsible steward. More importantly, he wants to ensure that his ideals and his practices are in sync. As he says, his household is like any private corporation—it will not survive if it is not clear about its purpose and its priorities. I have come to believe that he is right.

So now, when I am counseling couples who are preparing to solemnize their union, I routinely ask them what the mission of their household is going to be. This question invariably causes surprise and some confusion. I usually get one of two answers, or both. The first goes like this: "We plan to save money to buy a house wherever both of us are able to advance in our careers. At that point, if the timing is right, we'll have (or adopt) three children. Otherwise we'll wait." But sometimes I get this: "We don't have a mission. We just want to be together." In other words, the couple either responds with some version of a life-plan (which it is presumably the mission of the household to support and make possible), or with the assertion that the relationship is its own *raison d'être.*

The first response assumes that the household is merely a private institution that exists to serve the needs of its members. It fails to acknowledge that households also have a public face, and that they are ultimately accountable to the larger community. The second response leaves the household out of account altogether, because it assumes that true love can unfold without forging a place for itself in the world and without having some impact on the world, for good or ill.

I never fault any couple for either answer. Each reflects the tendency of our culture to regard true love as a union that absolves us, if only temporarily, from a host of other obligations, and which, even when those obligations must be tended to, presents itself to us as a refuge, a place of respite from the world. The second response more clearly reflects this bias. The couple has no mission, apart from their own desire not to be intruded upon. But the first response implies this, too. To some extent, it subordinates the household to worldly goals, so that even parenting is timed accordingly. But it assumes that the ultimate goal is not engagement with the world. The "mission" of the household is to promote sufficient worldly success to buy some separation from the world—a house in a "safe" neighborhood, with the "right" neighbors. Even when—as is usually the case with the couples I counsel—there is a genuine desire to create a household that includes children and that reaches out to include relatives and friends, the entire enterprise is viewed as something fundamentally inward-turning.

True Love Propels Us into the World

My constant agenda throughout this book is to counteract this bias. True love propels us into the world, not away from it. We must avoid the kind of thinking that pits the household against the world, or that so closely identifies household life with private life, that the *neighbor,* who meets us by and large outside our comfort zone, becomes, along with the vicissitudes of our work life, something the household is supposed to shield us from. I am not denying that a union requires some privacy to flourish, but it is absurd to imagine that human beings can carve out for themselves a safe haven of interaction that does not belong to the world. In our relationships we constitute the world in all its promise and menace, however private or restricted those relationships may be. Even in private we are in public, so long as we are in the same room with someone else. And we all know that the relative privacy of the home can make it a place of danger as well as a refuge.

The hidden side of any family can harbor terrible violence and hide problems that would be addressed if they could be seen. Abuse is as likely to happen domestically as in a back alley or on the battlefield, just as the love and nurture we celebrate when it flourishes in the household is also found in those same alleys and on the battlefield. Couples that hope their relationship will be sacred can themselves be signs of hope in the world, reminders that the world bears within itself the seeds of genuine love. The world needs such couples to be present and vocal about who they are and what they seek to achieve.

Best Practices

With that in mind, I would like to offer three "best practices" that in my view are essential to the institutional well-being and corporate effectiveness of a sacred union. These are (1) owning everything in common, (2) holding out for consensus in decision-making, and (3) giving as much as possible away.

Hold All Things in Common

Aside from sex, there is no more powerful demonstration that two people have given themselves to each other than joint ownership of everything they have. This is the outward and visible sign that they no longer claim property rights over themselves—their bodies, their goods, their reputation, their time. This sounds uncomfortably like slavery, and this discomfort may not be lessened all that much by the fact that this enslavement is voluntary and reciprocal. It is right that we should be troubled by this comparison, since slavery is an institution born in violence and sustained by contempt, and to enter into it voluntarily is a wrongful devaluation of one's own dignity as a child of God.

We must not shy away from thinking through what is really entailed in the notion of giving oneself away, but there other models for this that are equally radical but less problematic. Consider Francis of Assisi giving the clothes off his back and all his money away to beggars in the public square. This was not merely a divestiture of worldly baggage; its logical conclusion was self-donation, since what Francis ultimately aspired to was to be completely available to everyone, even the most despised. Was this enslavement? Certainly not, because Francis never gave up his freedom, which was the freedom to continue to offer himself as new occasions arose. This freedom is the key to understanding what is happening when two lovers give themselves to each other. The surrender of all worldly goods, and even of one's body, is not the relinquishing of one's freedom—not if the goal is to be as effectively present to one's partner as possible. The act of self-giving continues throughout the life of the union; this act, renewed daily, *is* the life of the union. Relinquishing one's claim to private property within that relationship simply makes it easier for that perpetual self-donation to occur.

I believe this is how it was in the early Church as well. Acts 3:44 recounts how the first Christians pooled their resources and owned everything in common. Luke offers us no rationale for this practice; he just reports it. But, given Luke's repeated references to the unity the early Christians enjoyed, it seems obvious that this experiment in communism was intended not only to demonstrate the young Church's unity to the world, but to create the conditions for complete interdependence and fellowship. Obviously, the Church could not sustain these conditions for long, if indeed it ever achieved them. But traditional Christian marriage and monasticism have always aspired to the ideal of common ownership, and it may well be that monastic and coupled households provide the only situations in which common ownership can be fully lived out.

The importance of this ideal for sacred unions cannot be overestimated, since, from a biblical point of view, their entire legitimacy rests in the fact that they constitute a lifelong exercise in self-giving. Practically speaking, this means a shared checking account and all assets under both names. It also means no prenuptial agreements: these simply guard against possible breakup by rendering all common ownership of goods provisional. I recognize the risk here. Unions do fall apart, and partners do abuse the trust that is placed in them. But if there is real fear of that happening *before* the union is entered into, then plans for formalizing the union should be cancelled, or postponed until these concerns can be resolved.

There is, of course, a vast difference between Christian teaching about marriage and the way women have been treated over the centuries in Christian countries. Women have often been regarded as the property of their husbands, and the marriage service as a rite of conveyance. In contrast, Thomas Aquinas, perhaps the most influential medieval interpreter of Christian doctrine, summed up marriage as follows: "Marriage consists essentially in an inseparable union of souls, husband and wife pledging unbreakable loyalty to each other for the purpose of bearing and bringing up children."[6] It can be argued that Thomas's sole focus on procreation diminishes the freedom of women, because it goes hand in hand with narrowing the role of married women to childbearing. Nevertheless, his emphasis on a partnership grounded in mutual loyalty speaks to the dignity of both partners.

Decide All Things Together

This brings us to the second "best practice": decision-making by consensus. One reason consensus is important is that it is the only practical hedge against the temptation for one partner to take advantage of the fact that the other partner has handed over all his autonomy. Agreeing to decision by consensus is not the same thing as acquiescence, which is what can happen when one is overcome by love, or just tired of arguing. Finding consensus involves flushing out disagreements, and then finding real resolutions to them, whether that be compromise or some new way that opens up. This is not to say that consensus is merely a check on the abuse of power. Consensus expresses the union of mind and heart that accompanies the union of body. Functionally, it is the same thing as both partners giving their lives to each other.

When Paul asked the church at Philippi to be of one mind (Philippians 2:5–6), he was asking them to present a united front to the world. But the example he gave for this is the self-emptying of Christ. In other words, working to achieve a common mind involves the foregoing of all self-interest. The question is how to do this without letting go of one's perspective on truth. The key is to remember that giving over one's life is not the same thing as giving over one's mind. Each partner owes the other the use of his critical faculties. And in fact, when we give our lives over to the beloved (in express imitation of Jesus, who emptied himself for our sake, taking on the form of a servant), our minds are freed to pursue truth without any thought to our own advantage, thus giving us all the more acumen and breadth of perspective to bring to our discussions.

This is all well and good, but do we not, in our self-giving, run the risk of substituting the beloved's advantage for our own, and thus inviting the same old self-interested approach to truth in through the back door? Not if we keep in mind that love of neighbor is not the same thing as annexing our neighbor, or offering oneself to be annexed by him. When I offer myself to my neighbor as a servant, I do so in the name of neighbor-love, and with the proviso that any service I am asked to render will be consonant with neighbor-love. Thus, a critical edge is built into my service from the beginning. I am not called to promote my neighbor's advantage over against others, but to honor him as a child of God. There will always be difficult and sometimes tragic occasions when my obligation to my beloved, or to my children, requires me to choose to help them and so not to help someone else. This is not because I am committed to pursue their interest at the expense of other people; it is because, when we have to engage in moral triage, our obligation lies with those who are closest and, over the long haul, depend most upon us.

In any case, when I enter into a union with someone, I don't check my brain at the door, I don't assume that my partner is always right, and I certainly don't seek her advantage at the expense of others, unless it is a matter of life and limb and the immediate circumstances force me to make a choice between helping her and helping someone else. What I must do, above all, is remain committed to the truth. Submission to the beloved should be the same thing as submission to the truth. When both parties approach their decision-making on that basis, what can emerge is, indeed, a common mind that is expansive, inventive, and productive in the cause of love, not just for the couple, but for everybody.

Give as Much as You Can

This brings us to the third essential practice: supporting those who have less than we do. This practice is called *Tzedakah* within Judaism, and *Zakat* in Islam, words that literally mean "righteousness." The closest equivalent within Christianity is "works of mercy" or "charity," the word for love applied more specifically to helping those in need. In these, as in all religions, giving generously to the poor, without making distinctions between individuals or groups and without imposing special restrictions, is an obligation laid on everyone. This obligation has a special bearing on couples, because it is the only way in which a couple can demonstrate that the love they bear toward each other is grounded in a fundamental commitment to the neighbor as such.

Two issues are at play here. On the one hand, if the mission of a sacred union is to witness to the love of neighbor, then that witness needs to be continually visible over long expanses of time. On the other hand, however much a couple's true love for each other may include the whole world of neighbors in its scope, it is always easy for the relationship to turn inward. This can happen because the couple succumbs to the prevailing assumption that romance offers an escape from neighbors and their demands. But it can even happen when a real household has been formed. As I have suggested, the household that arises from a sacred union may be thought of as a corporation whose mission is service. So it is the quintessential not-for-profit organization. But even the best nonprofits sometimes confuse success with survival at any cost, because, even more than individual people, corporations by their very nature are oriented toward continuity. So it may be for a household: it may be founded on the principle of neighbor-love, but become caught up in ensuring its own continuity without reference to anything that transcends it. The practice of charity provides an institutional antidote to this tendency ("Where your treasure is, there will your heart be also").

Sacred unions are grounded in mutual affection. But they also must become grounded in common purpose. It is in this second sense that they are like corporations, and it is here that they run into the temptation that dogs every corporation: placing collective purpose above ordinary human obligations. Just as corporations (whether profit or nonprofit) can place their own survival ahead of moral considerations (and can do so on ostensibly moral grounds—"we have the interests of our shareholders to uphold"), so couples who have made a life commitment may allow their loyalty to each other to trump the ideals that supported their union in the first place.

But I think the practice of charity does more than that. It provides the union with a way to participate in and influence the wider economy of which it is a part. Very early in the Church's history, the topic of rich and poor within the Church surfaced as a major issue. How were those with more means to relate to those who had less?

An answer eventually emerged: The rich were to support the poor materially, and the poor were to pray for the rich. The point was that the poor were automatically closer to God because of God's special love for the poor, but the rich could function as ongoing suppliers of material goods. The rich should not necessarily cease to be rich, but if they stayed rich, they should shepherd their resources so that they became a constant source of income for the poor.[7] John Wesley, speaking in the eighteenth century primarily to aspiring new members of the middle class, used this ancient model to encourage his hearers to gain the means to become charitable

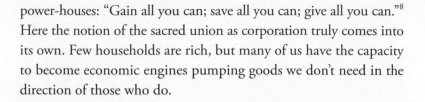

power-houses: "Gain all you can; save all you can; give all you can."[8] Here the notion of the sacred union as corporation truly comes into its own. Few households are rich, but many of us have the capacity to become economic engines pumping goods we don't need in the direction of those who do.

1. What do you do on major "family" holidays? Do you trade off years going between your families? Do you try to see both families on each holiday? Do you ever take a year off just for yourselves and the family you're building in your sacred union? Is your holiday pattern an intentional choice, or is it the result of "pressure" from your families of origin? How can you make more intentional choices in matters involving the families you are each part of?

2. Do you want your children (if you plan on having or adopting any) raised in a faith community? (Don't presume this to be an "obvious" answer; be sure you're making a decided choice.) Into which faith community? How will you decide this question?

3. What do you think about the "best practices" outlined in this chapter? Do you already live into these as a couple? Where do you fall short? How do you or don't you want to incorporate these into your life together?

Exercise:

Together create a "mission statement" for your household. After you've agreed upon this mission statement, set it aside for a few days, then come back to look at it more closely. Work together to decide how your mission as a family meets up (or fails to meet up) with your values, beliefs, and desires in this world. Working together once again, recreate your mission statement into a workable foundation for your union.

SIX

Being Parents

WHEN OUR FIRST CHILD, MAGDALENE, WAS BORN, IT SEEMED like the universe was there to help us. I was a graduate student at Oxford, and we were living in a tiny apartment in married student housing. Although Margaret had suffered for nine months from morning sickness, her pregnancy had gone without a hitch, and a team of midwives, along with graduate-student friends and members of the cathedral congregation, had looked after both of us so attentively that it never seemed as if we were on our own, even though we were very far from home. On the night of the birth, Pippa, one of the midwives, came by the apartment about nine o'clock in the evening. It was early July and still daylight. Margaret had been in labor for a while. Pippa told me to call her if there were any problems, and otherwise to show up at the hospital at eleven o'clock. So at the appointed time I called a taxi (which on our income we had never done in England), and shortly after eleven o'clock we were on our way to the John Radcliffe Hospital in a huge old hansom cab with a very solicitous driver.

By three o'clock the next morning, we had a daughter. Pippa washed her, weighed her, wrapped her in a receiving blanket, and laid her on Margaret's stomach. And then—I will never forget this—she asked if she might say a prayer of thanksgiving, which of course we were glad for. The next thing I remember is standing in the waiting room at four o'clock, phoning Margaret's parents and mine. Through the plate glass windows I saw that the day was already dawning. Three hours later, with Margaret and Magdalene safely ensconced in the maternity ward, I made my way home. As I stepped out of the main entrance to the hospital, there was our same cab driver, just letting someone off. So he took me home, and listened to me relate the whole night's drama. I was excited, proud, effusive. Then came the moment when I walked into the apartment, looked around, sat down, and began to sob uncontrollably. Partly it was exhaustion, partly relief. But I remember vividly thinking, "What am I going to do now?" What had crashed in on me was the overwhelming realization that I was now a father, and that Margaret and I were actually completely responsible for another life. All the help in the world would not change that. We had become parents.

Parenthood as Vocation

I tell this story to remind myself that being a parent can be a terrifying prospect, and rightly so. Usually the joys and the satisfactions outweigh the burdens, but the burdens are real, and they may well prompt us to ask why we should have children, given the choice. Before contraception was an easy option, the question might have seemed meaningless. If a man and a woman had sex together, they could expect to produce children as a result. But now, for opposite-sex as well as for same-sex couples, it is an option to forego parenthood. So the question is worth asking, if for no other reason than that parenting can now be approached as a vocation to which a couple may or may not be called. After much soul-searching, a couple may come to the conclusion that they are definitely not called to parenthood. On the other hand, I have had conversations with couples whose decision not to have children arises from considerations of convenience rather than call. In these cases I encourage them to consider that parenthood may be a vocation and a ministry that should not be avoided. This may be especially important in a

Christian context—not because Christianity places a heavy stress on parenting but because, historically, Christianity has not always accorded the task of child-rearing the honor it deserves. Certainly, there is an ambivalence about this in early Christianity. The fourth-century Greek theologian and spiritual writer Gregory of Nyssa associates procreation with the cycle of birth and death, which he says we should avoid participating in if at all possible. His North African contemporary Augustine tilts in this direction, too.[9] This all has to do with the prevailing prejudice in the ancient world against embodiment, which went hand in hand with distaste for marriage and a general suspicion of too much involvement with other people. But that is not a strain of Christianity I want to have anything to do with. The true heart of the Gospel is engagement with the neighbor, and sacred unions are a vocation arising out of that embrace. One important way in which that embrace is extended is by receiving children into our homes and our lives.

Parenthood as an Extension of True Love

Still, since there are many heterosexual couples who would disagree with Gregory of Nyssa yet still choose not to have children, the question remains: Why procreate? One answer is that people want to take part in the chain of the generations, by producing children out of their own bodies. This would explain why so many couples go to extraordinary lengths to become biological parents, rather than to adopt. But there is another important motivation for becoming a parent—one that involves no dynastic aspirations, and applies to adoption as well as procreation. Parenting is a dimension of adulthood. I am considering adulthood not merely as a function of age or as a characterization denoting a certain set of skills and abilities. Adulthood also names a set of conditions and experiences which are important components of a happy life. For many people, one of those components is the opportunity to nurture and guide children and young people. There are many ways to do this besides becoming a parent, but I am sure this is a major reason that many people do choose to become parents, whether biologically or by adoption. I am suggesting, in other words, that wanting to be a parent is closely related to wanting to be a teacher. Effective teaching at any level requires great skill, but my hunch is that the desire to impart general knowledge and pass on the fruit of personal experience is universal, and that the urge to be a parent often goes hand in hand with it.

Bringing out the relationship of parenting to teaching highlights the fact that parenting, like romantic love, is a form of neighbor-love. Teachers know that they are giving their students all the resources and knowledge they need to equal their teachers and surpass them. Likewise, parents share everything they have and are with their children, in order that they may eventually partake in their adulthood and, in the end, take their parents' place in the world. Unlike romantic love, parenting does not culminate in union. Its goal is to enable children to head out on their own. But like romantic love, it calls for a measure of self-giving that is on a par with the self-giving of true love.

Does this mean that couples should become parents if at all possible? This is a complicated question. I have suggested that serving other neighbors is a natural outgrowth of true love, because loving the neighbor in one instance leads to loving all neighbors. Perhaps couples who are able *should* become parents, either through procreation or adoption, if it is in fact the case that parenthood, like service, is a corollary of true love.

Our discussion of householding in chapter five also seems to point in this direction. As we saw there, a household comprises all the established patterns of interaction, the traditions of celebration and mourning, the rules and expectations, and, if you will, the *style and culture* that a couple develop for themselves over time, often starting long before they live together. Like any institution, it takes on a life of its own, so that very often the household is interacting as much with one or both of the partners as they are with each other.

Because the household is larger than the union that gives rise to it, it is able to integrate other persons into it. A couple cannot invite others into its union, but it *can* invite others into its household. If it can do this, *should* it not do this, given its original grounding in the love of neighbor? And what more natural way for a couple to invite the stranger into its midst than to welcome a child? This challenge applies equally to those who are capable of procreation and those who are not. Adoption is always an option for a couple, and there are couples who can procreate but choose also to adopt, or *solely* to adopt. Adoptive parenthood is a vocation of the highest order.

As I mentioned above, I have heard arguments against having children (either by adoption or procreation) that strike me as selfish: "We want to have more income to spend on ourselves." "We're content with what we have to offer each other—another person would just change the dynamic." "We cannot both pursue our careers and take time out for having children." It is hard to square these excuses with the love of neighbor. The concern about careers does have some legitimacy, if what is at issue is the fair sharing of responsibility for bringing up the child. But if we grant that both parents should bear the burden of parenting equally—and this goes for gay and lesbian parents as well—the issue of selfishness remains to be dealt with.

Is Parenthood a Calling in Your Relationship?

Still, I am reluctant to suggest that any couple is obliged to take on parenthood. All true lovers are obliged to render service to others besides each other, but if their situation and calling does not make service in the form of parenting a good option, there are many other ways to reach out to others. Yet this is what I would say to any couple in a position to raise children safely and properly: If you have the desire to be parents, go with it. There comes a time when it is becomes counterproductive to worry too much about timing, money, and career. There is no "right time" to receive a child into the household. The advent of a child is always intrusive and destabilizing, no matter when it comes—so better, I say, to plunge in and let the adventure begin. Sometimes I think young couples are unrealistically concerned to sequence their lives in an orderly fashion, forgetting that their initial love for each other was anything but orderly. Each was for the other a disorienting if blessed intrusion. Welcoming a child into their midst keeps godly disorientation in the picture.

Gay and lesbian couples face their own challenges when it comes to becoming parents, of course. Since they cannot produce offspring on their own, they must either adopt or produce a child biologically with the help of a third party. Adoption is an extremely difficult process for heterosexual couples; it can be an impossibility for gay or lesbian couples, depending what state or country they live in. It is usually easier for them to bring a child to birth with the help of a donor or a surrogate mother. But even this involves a loss of privacy most heterosexual couples don't have to put up with, not to speak of the legal complications that may attend their attempt to claim the child as their own. Given all this, I would not press a same-sex couple to pursue parenting (unless there is already a child from a previous relationship). But I want to underscore that if two women or two men have formed a lifelong union, any inclination they may have to be parents is no less an outgrowth of their love for each other than that of a man and a woman. It may be harder for them to become parents, but this does not mean that they shouldn't *want* to be parents and pursue all appropriate means to do so.

Same-Sex Parents

Sometimes it is argued that it is inconsistent to be gay and to want to bring forth children, as if one were mixing the unnatural with the natural. But in fact sexuality and the yearning to bring forth young cannot be linked in so mechanical a way—it is not as if heterosexuality goes hand in hand with wanting to beget children, while homosexuality does not. This is especially not so when we are talking about two persons who have given themselves to each other. Their sexual relations take up and amplify everything that is implied in union—including the raising of children. It is not the biological relationship between sex and procreation that produces the desire to be a parent with one's partner. Unless one seeks parenthood for selfish or immature reasons, the desire arises from the need for an objective correlative for the love one has for one's partner—a way, if you will, for that love to overflow. Traditional Jewish and Christian reflection on God's motive in creating the universe has pointed to the overflow or excess of God's love. So it is when two people have given themselves to each other. Whether they are a heterosexual or a same-sex couple, there is an excess of love that seeks a proper object beyond the couple.

The question still remains of how same-sex couples are going to become parents, apart from adoption. I would rule out insemination by way of sexual intercourse categorically, because it violates the vow of fidelity, and any attempt to argue that such a sex act would be purely instrumental demeans sex and falsely supposes that sex can be impersonal. The other possibilities all boil down to some combination of artificial insemination by a donor (anonymous or not) and the carrying of the fetus by a surrogate mother. For a lesbian couple, this would mean one of the partners' eggs being fertilized by sperm from a male donor. For a gay couple, this would mean a surrogate mother who might or might not also be the egg donor. Both these methods have been storm centers of ethical controversy for over two decades. How are they to be assessed by couples who cannot procreate without them?

On the face of it, there is nothing wrong with artificial insemination. It is not a depersonalizing of the sex act, because it is not a sexual act at all, and it does not depersonalize the conception any more than it would if, within a heterosexual marriage, the sperm of the husband were to be artificially introduced into the wife (this is a common procedure in the treatment of infertility). The real question is whether it is all right for a third party to be introduced into the picture. What does it mean for a man to be the biological parent of a child born to a lesbian couple? What does it mean for a woman to be the biological parent and/or the bearer of a child born to a gay couple? The stakes are further raised when we consider that these third parties should not be anonymous, if for no other reason than that the child has the right to know his or her genetic background. Third-party procreation at one remove raises the same concern as insemination by a third party through sexual intercourse. In the latter case, it is clear that a third party has intruded (or been welcomed) into the union in such a way as to violate the very foundation of the union. Is that the case with artificial insemination as well? I don't think so, because in this case the third party remains at one remove, never engaging sexually with one of the partners and perhaps never even appearing on the scene.

Nevertheless, these third parties stand in a special relationship to the child, and that relationship needs to be acknowledged and allowed to take its natural course. If at all possible, parents and children need to know everything about the child's biological origin, if for no other reason than that information about one's genetic inheritance factors into choices regarding health and lifestyle. Just as importantly, perhaps, we need to recognize that no human act is impersonal. Every interaction we have is personal, however "objective" we seek to be.

If I lay off a member of my staff, I can point to the need for a leaner workforce, but I cannot thereby hide the fact that I have made a decision that has an impact on a fellow human being's life. I must own that connection and not shrink from it. But the same is true of supposedly impersonal interactions that seem more positive. When I give money to a cause that seems worthy to me but also distant from me (let's say hunger relief in sub-Saharan Africa), I am nevertheless entering into a relationship that is personal: If those who have benefited from my donation decide to call on me, I have an obligation to acknowledge my connection to them. It's like the old proverb: If you save someone's life, you are theirs forever. There is no such thing as an impersonal connection with anyone, since any connection whatsoever surfaces the fundamental fact that we are already connected to one another, whether we like it or not. So if I donate my sperm to help a lesbian couple I don't know to bring a child into the world, I had better be ready to answer the door when that child knocks on my door as an adult, wanting to know who I am.

All of which is to say, although it is important to weigh matters like artificial insemination and surrogacy as carefully and as objectively as possible, it is also important to remember that real people are living out these scenarios and facing these moral questions. Sometimes the people most easily forgotten are the potential parents themselves, and their relationship to each other. When I discuss parenting with a couple, I am chiefly concerned that a couple tend their covenant with each other carefully, recognizing that if that covenant is—or even feels—violated in any way, it is far less likely to bear good fruit in the world. I have known couples so desperate to become parents that they forget their primary obligation to each other: they become careless of each other's thresholds of anxiety in their impatience to pursue now one option, now another. Parenthood by most means (adoption, procreation, third-party donation) is in most cases a worthy goal for two people who have committed themselves to the discipline of lifelong partnership. But the health and vitality of the partnership is crucial here. If the integrity of the partnership is compromised, so is the parenting that results from it.

Incorporating Children into Your Relationship

Let's turn now to a consideration of the work that parents take on once their child has arrived. I want to start by drawing attention to a temptation that arises for almost any couple facing being parents for the first time. Each partner must take care that the parent-child relationship is not in competition with the partner-partner relationship. This kind of competition can easily develop when one of the parents is dissatisfied with the primary relationship, and focuses all his or her affection on the child. But it can also arise when the relationship of the two partners is in good shape. As I have noted, the self-giving involved in being a parent is as intense, in its own way, as the self-giving that joins partner to partner. The parent, no less than the lover, gives herself or himself over unilaterally.

Indeed, the unilateral aspect of self-giving is even more striking in parenting, because there is no expectation of an answering act of self-giving. The command to honor our parents suggests that we owe quite a lot to our parents in return for their love, but we should note that this command, like all of the Ten Commandments, is addressed to us as adults, not children. As adults we owe a great deal to our parents. It is our duty to take their advice seriously, and to do everything within our power not to grieve them. Above all, it is our duty to ensure that they are safe and cared for in their old age.

Nevertheless, where infants, young children, and teenagers are concerned, parental love may sometimes be one-way love. Children are capable of great love, but eliciting such love cannot be the motive for parental love. Parental love is fundamentally sacrificial. That means that when their child is hostile or distant, parents are not off the hook: they must keep on loving. Most parents understand this very well. But the very fact that the parent's love for the child is so one-sided confers on it a moral and emotional energy that can for a time outshine the parent's relationship with his or her partner.

This should come as no surprise. Love of neighbor is all about self-giving without thought of return, and it is manifestly easier for a parent to love a child than for a partner to love a partner in this way. This is why the temptation to give the parental relationship priority over the original union is so strong. But it must be resisted, because the consequences are harmful, both for the child and for the couple. When one parent feels closer to the child than to the partner, something very much like a love triangle is set up. Even though sex is not involved, the parent who is left out feels like the victim of unfaithfulness. Meanwhile, once the child is old enough, it finds itself in an impossible position. Either it is defending its special relationship with one parent over against the other, or it is trying to broker a rapprochement between them.

The solution, of course, is for the couple to share the parenting as much as possible. I am not suggesting that parental tasks be distributed as evenly as possible. Although that's not a bad thing, it may be logistically impossible, given the vagaries of work schedules and other obligations. It is far more important to ensure that each parent has a role in at least one ritual of daily life.

With infants and preschoolers, this round of rituals usually includes wake-up and breakfast, shopping or playground, lunch, a nap, time with other children, dinner, and bedtime. When children are older, the major moments when parental involvement really counts are leaving for school (or being taken there), being picked up from school, family dinner, and bedtime. If a parent's work schedule makes it impossible to be around for any of these events, then it would be well worth it to consider changing jobs. Sometimes economic hardship makes this impossible, but if it's just a matter of making enough money rather than a lot of money, it is a mistake to choose the latter.

The only way to be part of your child's life is to be present every day, and present in such a way that your child has your full attention. But this alone is not enough to ensure that the relationship of the couple remains healthy and strong. When I say that the couple must share their parenting as much as possible, I mean that they must talk about it together every day, worry about it together every day, and make decisions relating to it together every day. There is absolutely nothing wrong with the relationship of partner-to-partner becoming utterly consumed by parenting, as long as this provides the medium whereby the union into which they have entered finds expression.

Preserving the Relationship

Still, even here there is a danger to be avoided. There is no harm in a couple spending their waking hours discussing their child. There *is* harm if none of that time is time spent alone, in relative privacy. The greatest gift a couple can give to their child is the permanence and resilience of their love for each other. But the maintenance of a healthy relationship is hampered if the parents have no space—not from each other, but from the child. Parents have to put their own commitment to each other ahead of their availability as parents. This seems counterintuitive, since, as we've noted, parenting is all about unilateral self-giving. But the proper subject of this self-giving is the couple, not each individual. No good is served if the union of the parents withers away for want of tending.

This was brought home to me early in our marriage. We had recently moved from England to the United States with three-week-old Magdalene, and I was settling into my new job as chaplain of an Episcopal high school in Los Angeles. By now our daughter was three months old and, if we were lucky, she would fall asleep in my arms around seven o'clock in the evening and sleep until she needed to be fed again, around one o'clock in the morning. This meant that Margaret and I finally had some time to ourselves, and could even expect a little sleep later in the evening. But we couldn't count on this. Every third night or so, I would lay our sleeping baby gingerly down in her crib and slide hopefully away, only to be summoned back by her wailing. So the cycle would start all over again: I would walk around with her in my arms until she dozed off, and then try to put her down. Sometimes that process, repeated seemingly endlessly, took us right up to the one o'clock feeding time, when she would finally succumb to a deep sleep. Still, there were enough "good" evenings, as we called them, that we thought we could risk having someone over to dinner.

There was a new assistant headmaster who had arrived about the time we did, ahead of his wife and four children, who were going to join him as soon as their house on the east coast sold. So John was on his own, we really liked him, and we rightly assumed that he was used to navigating dinner time with a three-month-old. John came over about six o'clock, and we chatted and had hors d'oeuvres, and after Margaret fed Magdalene, John took turns with me walking her around until she fell asleep. I carried her carefully to her room. She did not wake up when I slipped away, and the three adults sat down to our meal. No sooner had we started but the wailing started up. As I was getting up from my chair to get Magdalene, John said, "Why don't you just let her cry?" I sat down again.

"What do you mean, just let her cry?"

"I mean," said John, "you'll never be able to count on an evening together if you don't teach her that going to bed means staying in bed. Just let her cry—I don't mind it at all. If you can stand it, you'll have established a limit that is essential for her good, and for yours and Margaret's."

We were astonished. It had never occurred to us that we could *just let her cry.* She did cry for an excruciating fifteen minutes, but then she stopped and slept, and we had a wonderful time with John. I do not intend to imply that this bedtime tactic, commonly referred to as "crying it out," is a practice that should be followed by all parents. Parenting experts and manuals have varying opinions of the practice—and this book is not a parenting manual. I use the example here to illustrate the importance of making ample space for the partner-partner relationship. Each couple must find its own ways to create this space. Nevertheless, I remember this evening with great fondness, not only because it was a turning-point for us as parents (Magdalene never refused to go to bed again), but because we never had another chance to develop the friendship. John became very ill a few months later and did not survive through the school year. I will always be grateful to him for teaching us that we had to look out for our marriage for Magdalene's sake as well as ours.

As the Children Grow . . .

Partners need to ensure that the integrity and priority of their relationship continues as their children grow older. But as time goes on, the challenge has less to do with finding time together alone, and more to do with managing to present a united front to their children. Once our second child, Lucy, came along, it wasn't long before both girls became adept at trying to get what they wanted by playing me against Margaret, and vice versa. Children know their parents very well, and are expert at choosing the parent most likely to say yes to a given proposal, and the one most likely to say no.

The truth is that parents are quite likely to come to parenthood with differing thresholds of anxiety, differing notions of what is socially acceptable, and different criteria for deciding what is worth making an issue of and what is not. This is to be expected, since they themselves are the product of different families with differing approaches to child rearing. When I counsel couples preparing to enter into a formal union, I always ask them to talk with me about their approaches to child rearing, since it is very helpful to get possible conflicts in this area out onto the table ahead of time, so they can be acknowledged and perhaps resolved.

But some clashes will never emerge until one's child makes a specific request. When our ten-year-old child asked for permission to attend a sleepover on the night before Easter, it was a struggle for us to know how to respond. My wife and I both thought that it was important to preserve our identity as a committed Christian family; we also both feared turning our daughter against that identity by refusing her request. But the dilemma was complicated by the fact that we weighed these concerns differently. I don't remember which one of us was asked first about this, but I do know that Margaret and I decided that we would not allow our children to pressure us into making decisions until we had had the chance to discuss them thoroughly, *without the children present*. In our family this proviso became known as the "Committee for the Betterment of Life." Whether the deliberations of that committee bettered our life or not, I cannot say, but it certainly gave Margaret and me the space and the time we needed to sort out our differences and propose a response to our children that we could both live with.

Our Children Are Not Our Own

So far I have been focusing on the need to keep the parenting couple united and strong. But there is another way to look at all this talk about boundaries and united fronts. The parents may need to preserve their integrity over against their child, but boundaries are also necessary in order to preserve the child's integrity over against its parents. It is commonly said that our children do not belong to us, and that is true. The child is not an extension of its parents, but a new arrival, an immigrant from nowhere, received and taken on by its parents as a neighbor and fellow pilgrim. There is something to be said, therefore, for a certain amount of space between parents and children. Not a space that lessens the parents' complete responsibility for their child's safety—that is not in question—but a space that does not reject surprises out of hand and always anticipates the day when the child will pursue his or her path as an unsupervised adult.

I am not talking about surprises that would or should be alarming to anyone, as, for instance, the discovery that one's child is frequenting hate sites on the internet. I mean surprises that are not bad according to any objective standard, but may run afoul of a parental agenda. I don't need to enumerate the possible surprises—movies and novels are full of them. Sexual orientation, political partisanship, career choice, religious conversion—all these may alienate a teenager from his parents. But it is entirely up to the parents to produce the space in which their children can try on identities and explore possible vocations without feeling that they are putting their relationship with their parents at risk.

All of which is to say that we parents do not receive our children as gifts directed toward ourselves. Our role is to welcome and to initiate newcomers into the human community. How can parents best do this? If parenting is like teaching, the household into which we welcome a child is best understood as a classroom. Much of the schooling children and teenagers need in order to interact successfully with the world is delegated by the household to other organizations. But there is one area in which no school can substitute for the parents, and that is the introduction of the parents' own religious and moral beliefs and commitments. Parents often shy away from this role. They fear that by raising their children in a particular faith tradition, they are depriving them of the freedom to make their own independent faith decisions as adults.

This is simply not the case. If our children are to be initiated into the human race, they cannot be initiated into it in the abstract. There is no such thing as humanity in the abstract. There is only humanity as it has been shaped by particular convictions and traditions. The more securely a child is grounded in a particular tradition, the more confidently she can navigate the great ocean of human culture, and weigh what comes her way.

Parenthood and Faith

Sometimes the difficulty lies in the parents' uncertainty about their religious faith, or about the traditions that accompany it. In that case, the remedy is straightforward. Reconnect with your faith. Find a way to explore your questions about God. In part this means finding or rejoining a faith community, and doing what it takes to make a place for yourselves in it. This can be daunting, because many places of worship either are not particularly welcoming or expect the newcomer to take the initiative in showing up for classes and social events. But that is really no excuse for giving up and staying away. Establishing a real connection with a house of worship—and that means being known and recognized as a familiar presence—provides a base for household life that can be achieved in no other way, precisely because of the way congregations and households complement and reinforce each other.

But joining a congregation is only half the task. Parents also need to be in touch with the spiritual values and moral vision that drew them together in the first place, whether or not these are religious in the strict sense. They must find occasions to talk about these things with each other, so that they can imagine how they will talk to their children about them. What are the special days that need to be observed, the stories that need to be told, the sacred places that need to be visited, and the family traditions that need to be passed on? It is all too easy for couples to take their own sacred history for granted, and still easier to make no provision for that history to be communicated to the next generation. When people lived out their lives in the same community, a whole range of adults could be counted on to help with this. It is now largely up to the parents themselves to tell their children what they stand for.

How can this be done? For every couple and every household it will be different, but for most it will come about partly by design, partly by accident. For instance, Margaret and I decided early on that we would celebrate name days as well as birthdays. (In some Christian traditions, children are often named after saints. The name day is the feast day of the child's namesake.) We did not foresee how those celebrations would evolve, however. For instance, Lucy's name day falls on December 13th, and mine on December 21st. So both days became part of a steady march toward Christmas, beginning with St. Nicholas Day (December 6th), when we would fill the girls' shoes with chocolate coins (Hanukkah geld, readily available at this time of year, served this purpose very well!), continuing with Lucy Day, which is when the nativity scenes still go up, and Thomas day, when we always get our tree. Lucy's name day also functioned as a kind of yearly house blessing. Since Lucy means "light," we used to have her lead us from room to room through our cavernous apartment at General Seminary. In an admittedly odd importation from the ritual for the Vigil of Easter, Lucy would sing "The light of Christ" at each doorway, and we would enter the room singing "Thanks be to God!" This went on every year from the time Lucy was three until, at age eleven, she kindly but firmly put her foot down and refused to do this anymore.

I would hardly expect most households to go in so much for ritual. Even in our household, Magdalene's July name day has always simply been the occasion for a fancy cookout. Special days can be celebrated with special foods, gift-giving, a day at the shore—it hardly matters, as long as there is some regularity from year to year, and the reason for the day is explained and talked about. It is also common knowledge that having a family meal every day adds immeasurably to a child's sense of security and, especially in the teenage years, provides a casual—but regular—occasion for information to be exchanged and concerns to be raised and addressed. Such meals are also sacred rituals, no matter how ordinary or informal they are. There is no religious tradition that does not place the expression of mutual respect and love through the sharing food at the heart of its practice. I know of no more natural or effective way for parents to communicate their commitment to each other and to their children than for them both to sit down with their children evening after evening around the same table. Of course, there is no question that modern schedules militate against the regular family meal, and it only gets harder as the children get older. But just as I cannot exaggerate how important it is to build in at least one significant and predictable encounter with one's child each day, I also cannot stress the value of the family meal too much. It is worth switching jobs and saving less for college to make it happen.

Where Church and Household Embrace

I would like to conclude by saying something specific about Christian households. It has become almost fashionable in some circles to refer to the family as the "domestic church," largely because of its role in conveying Christian faith and practice to the next generation. I am uncomfortable with the term because it blurs the distinction between the household as an essentially private institution and the Church, which should be as public as possible. Still, when the New Testament refers to the whole Church as "the household of faith," it is drawing our attention to the fact that the household and the Church mirror each other in at least one way.

Both are schools in which we are learning how to love one another no matter what. In the household, we do this with just a few people—our partner and our children—but precisely because they are just a few, we can give ourselves to them with a degree of generosity that borders on the prodigal. In the Church, we are struggling to live out the love of neighbor with every neighbor, or at least with every member of the human community we may happen to come in contact with. But our weakness and spiritual poverty are such that most of us cannot even begin to offer ourselves with such generosity to our friends, let alone our acquaintances, and still less to strangers and enemies.

In the wider arena of the Church, we must content ourselves with achieving the disciplines of respect, patience, forgiveness, and tact: these we can learn to offer to all comers. Yet what the household offers in intensity, the Church makes up for in scope. What both have in common is the desire to be schooled in neighbor-love, one way or the other. Clearly, the Church is more analogous to a city than to a household, and is often referred to that way. But when it is spoken of as the household of faith, it is in recognition of the fact that the intensity and limitlessness of the love of partner for partner and parents for children sets the bar for Christian love: It is the ultimate standard for our relationships with everyone without exception.

In the Book of Acts, Luke summarizes the life of the early Church in this way: "They devoted themselves to the apostles' teaching and fellowship, to the breaking of bread and the prayers" (Acts 2:42). This can be read as a summary of life in a household grounded in Christ's love.

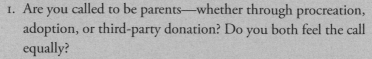

1. Are you called to be parents—whether through procreation, adoption, or third-party donation? Do you both feel the call equally?

2. Do you want to be parents (which is fundamentally a different question than one of calling)? Why or why not? What influences your decision either way? Are you in agreement on this?

3. Assuming that you wish to be parents by one means or another, what sort of parenting do you want to pursue? Will the chores and responsibilities be divided equally between you? What will you do if one or both of your careers come into conflict with your parenting responsibilities? How will you approach the challenges you will face in your relationship with each other, and your relationship with your children?

Exercise:

Each of you separately, on a sheet of paper, write down a word, phrase, or sentence that describes what you as an individual most want to pass down to your child. Share this with your partner and talk about it. Then, separately and on the same sheet of paper, describe what you hope to pass on as a couple. Share what you have written with each other, and discuss it. Keep track of these desires, referring back to them when difficulties arise in your journey as parents. Perhaps even consider keeping them to share with your children when they become adults and are considering a sacred union of their own.

SEVEN

When We Hurt Each Other

THE MARRIAGE SERVICE IN THE BOOK OF COMMON PRAYER includes the following prayer for the couple: "Give them grace, when they hurt each other, to recognize and acknowledge their fault, and to seek each other's forgiveness and yours." When I am officiating at a marriage, I sometimes sense surprise and a slight discomfort in the congregation at this point, as if the last thing they expected to hear about on such an occasion was couples hurting each other. But of course it is inevitable that we will behave badly, even to those we love.

I'm not talking here about abusive behavior. Physical or emotional violence has nothing to do with love, but rather registers hatred and contempt. I'll never forget the words of a guest psychiatrist on a talk show program on battered women: "If he hits you, it means he doesn't love you."

Conflict Is a Part of Sacred Union

What I mean—and what the Prayer Book has in mind—is ordinary, everyday unpleasantness: the petty, unkind acts we commit even against those we love, simply because we are self-centered and sinful. How many times have I been cross and grumpy at the dinner table because the sermon isn't finished or some other deadline is looming? Or dismissive of an opinion because it contradicts one of my favorite prejudices?

One of the tasks a couple faces early on is how to move through these minor failures honestly and quickly, so that they don't turn into something bigger. This takes being sufficiently self-aware to know one's own patterns of unpleasantness, to notice the behavior as it happens, and to say "I'm sorry" right away. All this needs to go hand in hand with a genuine attempt to correct the behavior, but some patience on the other partner's side is important too. A little kindly humor also helps. What needs to be avoided at all costs is the endless round of defensiveness and recrimination that almost certainly results when one party refuses to admit wrongdoing and the other is bent on catching the wrongdoer in the act. The point is, true love does not exempt any of us from human weakness. We bring that weakness into our unions and our households, and we should expect a significant portion of our life together to be spent working on confession, forgiveness, and reconciliation. This is perhaps the chief way in which a union achieves holiness over time, and a genuine initial commitment to this work is what lends a union whatever holiness it possesses at its outset.

Ambivalence and True Love

But here we run up against a problem that we need to face head-on. It seems to me that there are specific temptations to sinfulness that arise as a direct result of entering into a lifelong union. The commitment of one's life to another person is a massive decision. It calls for reserves of moral courage and selflessness that are beyond most of us to muster on our own. So when the ecstasy of falling in love gives way to the reality of lifelong promises and vows, the truest love may betray some ambivalence at its heart. For most couples preparing to take vows, this ambivalence is a taboo subject. The risk seems too great that the genuineness of their love will be called into question, or, worse yet, that one party or the other will disengage from the union for fear that the other's commitment can't be trusted.

But I think ambivalence about union is unavoidable. After all, true love is a frontal assault on self-centeredness. So it should come as no surprise that our own selfishness should rise up in self-defense to counteract true love. This is the dynamic Paul has in mind when he says that the law itself awakens sin, and that the same will that seeks to be in sync with God can also seek to run the other way: "For I do not do the good I want, but the evil I do not want is what I do" (Romans 7:19).

Since ambivalence is always present, and since there can be no doubt that it affects how partners relate to each other, sooner or later it needs to be put on the table as something that can be discussed. Otherwise couples deprive themselves of the means of getting to the bottom of the most serious hurts they inflict on each other. Such explorations are painful, but they are well worth the risk of disengagement if they can bring hurtful behavior under control and, still more importantly, strengthen and clarify the bonds of love uniting partners to each other. This chapter is an attempt to get that discussion going.

Fear

I see three basic sources for ambivalence about true love. The first is fear. There are all kinds of ways in which entry into a union can inspire legitimate fear. For some, loss of autonomy is the hardest thing to bear. This is especially challenging for people who have been single adults long enough to take total freedom in decision-making for granted. Giving up that freedom can feel like a small death. This is not just a question of making all major decisions in consultation with one's partner; in most cases it means a narrowing of options: less flexibility, less mobility, less ready cash.

For others, having to grow up is the fearful thing. Growing up has to do in part with claiming who one is once and for all. There are many facets to an identity: one's faith, one's vocation, one's way of relating to one's ethnicity, and one's past. Claiming a life-partner is just one of those facets. But if we are resisting being pinned down to a settled identity, then we may well be ambivalent about committing ourselves to a covenanted partnership—it's just one more tent-peg driven into the ground. Growing up also has to do with taking responsibility both for oneself and for others. Combined with a certain clarity about who one is, it makes for that peculiar mix of teaching and nurture that links adulthood so closely to parenting. Entering into a covenanted union signals one's willingness to claim responsibility for the safety and well-being of one's beloved, and of the children and others that may become part of the household over time. But since lifelong unions and the households they produce are the basic unit of the body politic, entering into such a unit also communicates readiness to take up one's responsibilities as a member of that larger body. This, too, can cause fear.

For others the fear may simply lie in being too well seen and too well known by one's partner. As we have seen, true love arises out of deep insight into the beauty and actual (or potential) goodness of the beloved. But such vision works in both directions. When the lover's love is returned by the beloved, the lover also becomes the object of the beloved's keen discernment. Sometimes it is hard for us to imagine that anyone who sees us clearly will find much there to celebrate. So we shrink from exposure—even exposure to the love of our life. This fear of being found out to be a fraud or a fool goes hand in hand with the fear that, despite our best intentions, we will fail as a partner—so better not even to try.

Finally, union may be fearful for some because it sets up the conditions for more bereavement in a life already too much acquainted with loss. Sometimes it seems better to avoid attachment rather than to set oneself up for grief.

Thankfully, most of us are free from at least some of these fears. Those of us who are afraid of settling down may at least enjoy a reasonable confidence in our self-worth; those of us who are afraid of loss may have no qualms at all when it comes to responsibility for others. But I think it is a rare person who is not fundamentally threatened in some way by the prospect of lifelong union with another. The threat may not prevent us from going forward, but, if we do not look at it squarely, it will bring with it an element of ambivalence into the relationship that can have harmful consequences. It's as if we enter into the union with our fingers crossed, hoping for the best. This is not to say that ambivalence amounts to a mental reservation—as if the vows are taken but the intention to keep them is not there. I think most of us take the covenant we make with our beloved with utmost sincerity, and intend to honor it. Nevertheless, unacknowledged fear binds us and holds us back from the unrestrained self-giving on which the well-being of the union ultimately depends.

Worse yet, unacknowledged fear leads to hurtful behavior. Human beings are relentlessly logical creatures. If an equation is lopsided, we even it out somehow. If we are ambivalent about the union we are in and do not admit it, we are very likely to communicate the ambivalence in other ways. The kind of behavior that communicates fear is fairly predictable.

We deal with real or perceived danger by running away or launching a counterattack. Abandonment and infidelity are classic examples of flight—not from a relationship that is bad but from a relationship that is viable, and hence scary for any or all of the reasons outlined above. Withdrawal into work or into friendships that preceded the union is more acceptable but still serious and potentially very harmful. As for counterattack (and remember, there has been no attack to begin with—this is just unacknowledged ambivalence playing itself out), the pattern is well known and reflected everywhere in novels, plays, and films. The lover who does not measure up to the beloved seeks a way out. Sometimes this comes in the form of a profession of unworthiness, but more often than not it is an attack on the beloved as in some way unworthy. This theme shows up everywhere in Shakespeare, where the presenting issue is jealousy, but the deeper issue is clearly the lover's sense of incompetence in the face of the beloved's superior virtue. (I am thinking here particularly of *Othello* and *A Winter's Tale*.) By impugning the worth of the beloved, the hostile lover rejects the initial vision of the beloved as false, and so clears the way for disengagement. In real life, the line between loyalty and rejection may be less clearly drawn, and actions intended to diminish the worth of one's partner may be more subtle, but they are not hard to spot, once we are looking for them.

Remarks about physical appearance ("Are you watching your weight?") or behavior in public ("I wish you wouldn't be so free with your opinions") are a sure sign that the dignity of the other partner is under attack. Such remarks come uncomfortably close to abuse in their disparagement. Indeed, if they coalesced into a regular pattern of attack, we would not hesitate to regard them as abusive.

Truth-Telling

So far we have been considering a form of ambivalence that is mostly associated with the period immediately preceding and following the exchange of vows. Fear is the enemy in the early days. But ambivalence often re-emerges later on in the relationship, as a result of one partner's resistance to the other's authority as a truth-teller. True love does not blind us to the beloved's complex mix of strengths and weaknesses, virtues and vices, areas of wisdom and areas of foolishness. In fact, it helps us see each other more clearly. This is why true love always has a critical edge: it has as much to do with truth (telling it as it is) as troth (remaining faithful, no matter what). So if my partner sees me pursuing a course that is harmful to myself or others, she is likely to be distressed by this, and to call me on it. Lifelong partners can and should play a prophetic and critical role for each other, which can include indignation and anger by the one against the other, for the other's sake. But what if I don't want to hear hard truths? Then my love for my partner is likely to be tempered by dislike for what she has to say.

Once again, ambivalence invariably finds expression in words and actions that hurt. To be in denial about the truth is to call the partner's prophetic authority into question. There are many ways to accomplish this, the simplest being to be so familiar with one's partner that anything like prophetic authority seems outsized and out of place. As the years go by, it is easy for partners to become sloppy or disrespectful in their communication with each other. Calling out from one end of the house to the other, not listening carefully, interrupting, teasing, using nicknames to address each other—these are all natural by-products of familiarity, and, just as familiarity is not bad in itself, nor are these. But if love's diction is always pitched low, so will be its horizon.

Thich Nhat Hanh reminds us that in the Buddhist tradition, spouses are expected to treat each other as guests, that is, with courtesy and solicitude. Jane Austen's novels provide a fascinating window into a time and set of social circumstances in which there was little to distinguish the civility accorded to a stranger in public and a family member in private. I cannot imagine addressing my wife as "Mrs. Breidenthal," nor do I wish to return to the rigid hierarchies that marked Austen's world. Still, attention to courtesy keeps us mindful of each other's dignity—and each other's role as truth-teller.

Casualness about relationships with one's partner can set the stage for real viciousness when the partner breaks the rules and calls us on something serious. If I think I can say anything I want, whenever I want, I am not likely to bridle my tongue when I feel under attack. I may retaliate against criticism by pointing out my partner's failings, thus abusing my own authority as prophet: "Who are you to tell me how I should act? Get your own house in order first." I may deny the fact that my partner knows me well enough to understand my reasoning and my needs: "You have no idea what it's like to be in my shoes." I can acknowledge the force of my partner's complaint and simply insist that I am incapable of meeting a higher standard: "You should have known better than to get hooked up with me." I can debase myself with no thought of amendment ("I don't see how you can even bear to live under the same roof with me") or, which is almost the same thing, I can blame my partner for being too good ("You ask too much; what ordinary mortal could bear to live with you?"). Finally, I can simply lie: "It's not true," or, "I've stopped."

Most unions survive the dynamics of fear, but many don't make it past the dynamics of denial. Fear subsides as we settle into the give-and-take of household life, but resistance to truth persists as long as we remain in denial about it, as does the distasteful and disrespectful behavior it inspires. No one can go on like that forever. Either the wayward partner begins to listen, or the union breaks up.

So what is the way forward when one partner hurts the other? Jesus says in Matthew 18 that the fault must be acknowledged, and forgiveness sought.

That is certainly a beginning. As I suggested above, each partner needs to get into the habit of admitting wrongdoing as soon as it happens. But remorse and confession are not enough to restore what has been lost. The wronged party must weigh in, and it should not be a foregone conclusion that things will proceed as if no hurt had occurred. Jesus tells his disciples that they have the power to bind and to loose, to hold people to the consequences of their sins or to free them to start afresh. This is essentially the power we all have over one another as neighbors, since we all have the freedom to be in fellowship or to refuse fellowship. The wronged party in a union has this power, too. He or she is free to judge whether or not the wrong committed by the partner precludes further fellowship.

What this comes down to is the decision whether to forgive or not. Forgiveness is a complex notion, however. Literally it means to give something over—normally, to give over what is owed to one. When we forgive, we cancel a debt—we let it go. Hannah Arendt,[10] a Jewish political philosopher who escaped from the Nazis and became a celebrated proponent of American democracy, rightly

Matthew 18 provides a fascinating analysis of the way in which the Christian community should balance judgment and forgiveness. If one member of the community harms another, the aggrieved party is required to speak to him or her privately, so that the matter can be resolved one-on-one. The clear implication is that reconciliation is the object. If that fails, the aggrieved party is to bring witnesses to a second conversation. If that fails, the whole community is brought in. In the end, if the perpetrator will not listen to the community, he or she is to be ejected from the community: "Let such a one be to you as a Gentile and a tax collector" (Matthew 18:17). But this exclusion is almost tongue-in-cheek. One of the main characters in Matthew's Gospel is Matthew himself, who was a tax collector when Jesus invited him to follow him. And Matthew's Gospel concludes with the risen Christ's commission to make disciples out of all the Gentiles (Matthew 28:19). So treating a wrongdoer like a Gentile and a tax collector is not exclusion at all: he or she becomes someone to be invited into fellowship with Christ. In other words, there can be no judgment in the Church that is not at the same time an occasion for renewed relationship. This point is underscored a little later in Matthew 18, when Peter asks Jesus how many times he must forgive someone who has sinned against him. "As many as seven times?" asks Peter. Jesus answers: "Not seven times, but, I tell you, seventy-seven times" (Matthew 18:21–22). Judgment is not the opposite of forgiveness, and justice is not the opposite of mercy. Being clear about wrongdoing must always include the offer of forgiveness. By the same token, forgiveness presupposes the clear and (if necessary) public expression of grievances. Matthew is not interested in keeping conflicts and grievances hidden.

noted that forgiveness is the key to any kind of common life, since without it we cannot get over past wrongs and work together for a better future. The willingness to forgive goes hand in hand with a commitment to neighbor-love. But understood in this broad sense, forgiveness does not necessarily offer hope for a broken union. It is a very good thing if a couple parting ways can do so forgivingly, and many do. Sometimes this is the best that can—or should—be hoped for. But if a broken or impaired union is to be repaired, a deeper kind of forgiveness is required—not just the giving over of a debt, but the giving over of oneself. Such radical forgiveness is nothing other than the unilateral self-giving that has constituted the true love of the wronged party from the outset.

I hesitate to encourage radical forgiveness, because all too often it is invoked to keep victims of abuse in range of their abusers. So let's be clear about when forgiveness is called for and when it isn't. Jesus says that we should love our enemies, but he does not say that we must enter into covenant with them. He does not even say that we must forgive them outright. Matthew 18:21–22 says that we must never put a cap on our forgiving, but this forgiveness assumes some recognition of fault on the other side. In any case, loving and forgiving are not the same thing. We can love unilaterally, and we are commanded to love without stint. In practical terms, we are to wish our enemies well, we are to pray for them, and we are to offer them material assistance. But we can do all this without losing sight of the fact that these are our enemies who have wronged us and who may well wrong us again.

Forgiveness is different. We cannot forgive unilaterally, and we are not commanded to do so. Because forgiveness is the canceling of a debt, it requires that the existence of the debt be acknowledged by both parties. It is not enough for me to claim that I have been wronged. The one who wronged me must admit wrongdoing. That is why it is so offensive when one person says to another, "I forgive you," without the other having confessed to anything. It is no less offensive to offer forgiveness when forgiveness is not asked for—even if the wrong itself is acknowledged. It is a different story when someone who has wronged me asks for my forgiveness. Then I must give it seventy times over. Why? Because the request for forgiveness implies a genuine desire to be reconciled, and an intention to act in accordance with that professed desire. Since Christianity is the religion of life from death, the possibility of a new beginning, we are bound to give every request for forgiveness a chance. But the ancient Church required periods of probation in which the genuineness of such requests could be tested: Lent has its roots in these times of testing. In the early Church, the period before Easter was a time when converts to Christianity were given the opportunity to learn more deeply what it meant to be a follower of Jesus, and to reject the Gospel if it placed demands on them that they were not willing or ready to bear. It was also a time when those who had been excluded from the Christian community could demonstrate their willingness to abide by the community's norms.

How can these complex teachings about justice and forgiveness inform our reflection on marital breakdown? Is it unchristian or unwise for the injured party within a union to impose appropriate penances: no sex for awhile, no easy companionship, no help with work? On balance I would counsel against such strategies. What is required is a measured approach to forgiveness that doesn't cut any corners but honors everyone's dignity, wronged and wrongdoer alike.

Self-Giving

There remains yet a third ground for ambivalence that may emerge far down the road, when a union has achieved real stability and maturity. When a union is successful, it sometimes happens that both partners are called to an even higher level of self-giving, one that entails the final burning away of every lingering fear of loss, every remaining pocket of untruth. This call may come in the form of a catastrophic illness, the death of a child, the loss of a job or a reputation. Or it may come with each partner's growing awareness that, after years of life together, both will drift apart if they do not go deeper. In all these cases, the familiarity and comfort both partners have achieved with each other is either upended or called into question. They are strangers again, and they have the choice of falling in love all over again at a higher rate of exchange, or of leading essentially separate lives under the same roof. Well might we be ambivalent in the face of such a choice! After years of living together, and years simply of living, who wants to re-engage the drama of romance, even if it is a drama pitched at a higher key?

It is not uncommon for tragedy to send an otherwise solid couple reeling or drifting toward marital breakdown. I will never forget a conversation I had with an older member of a parish where I was serving as a priest. I will call her Martha. I had first met Martha on a Sunday morning in Advent—there had been a flurry of excitement about her appearance in church. As the worship team waited in the wings for the organ prelude to give way to the processional hymn, several choir members explained that this woman and her family had at one time been pillars of the church, but had stopped attending some years back and then had moved away. Their son, then a senior in high school, had been killed by a drunk driver as he was crossing the street just blocks from their home. I had heard about this tragedy—it had come up in various ways since my arrival, and was clearly an event that had touched the parish deeply. The young man's parents eventually separated, and Martha returned home to pick up her life again in the church and neighborhood that she knew and loved so well. About a year after this, at the tail end of the coffee hour on a Sunday morning, Martha told me the whole story. After the accident, her husband couldn't bear to go to church anymore, and eventually insisted on moving to a different town where they could start over again. He had lost his faith and could not bear to set foot in the house of the God who had betrayed him. Nor could he bear passing day after day by the spot where his son had been killed. Martha stuck by her husband. She didn't want to leave him alone on Sunday mornings, so she didn't go to church anymore. She didn't want him to suffer, so she agreed to move to a new home in another town. But her own way of dealing with the loss of her son was completely different from her husband's. Martha was devastated, but, while her husband was losing his faith, hers was becoming deeper. She did not want to stop attending church, but she did not want to be disloyal to her husband, either. When the clergy of the parish and a number of parishioners called her to see how she was doing, she said she just needed some space. But when the space was given, she felt keenly that she had cut herself off from the one community that could sustain her in her loss. The eventual move away to a new house in a different town clinched her isolation. From this point on, her only focus was her husband, who was busy trying to build a new life that did not include the loss of his son. Not surprisingly, Martha and her husband grew apart. He could not bear to think about his son; she insisted on facing her son's death and integrating it into her life. In the end Martha left her husband and came home, so that she could take up her life again, with all its losses and all its openness to grace.

Taking up our lives again after traumatic loss may seem just too hard. Martha sticks in my mind because she was so strong and so forthright about her pain. But her willingness to engage her pain head-on, together with her deepening faith, placed her on a trajectory that led her away from her life-partner. Here, as in so many cases, a shared loss yielded separate journeys and final separation. Was this inevitable? This question has haunted me for years. As far as Martha and her husband are concerned, I will never know the answer. I am too far removed now, and never knew enough in the first place to discern whether things could have turned out differently. What I can say is this: couples that are coping with catastrophic loss—be it the loss of a child, of a livelihood, or of a home—must go out of their way to reconnect with each other. Different reactions to loss are to be expected. But if the partnership is to survive, these differences must be acknowledged. I suspect that Martha and her husband would have stayed together if they had been able early on to talk through their differing responses to the loss of their son. But any such conversation presupposes utter closeness. What is needed in the end is a concerted recommitment on the part of both partners *to each other*.

The Soul's Dark Night

Here we can borrow wisdom from the Christian mystical tradition. The call to fall in love with one's partner all over again bears a strong resemblance to a crucial stage in the soul's spiritual journey toward union with God. I am referring to what St. John of the Cross famously called the "dark night of the soul."

St. John of the Cross (1542–91), a close friend of St. Teresa of Ávila, joined her in leading a movement to reform the Carmelite Order, restoring its focus on a life of simplicity, withdrawal, and contemplation. He is best known for his exploration and analysis of the soul's ascent toward union with God, which he constantly depicts as the union of bride and bridegroom. Although his subject is our struggle to deepen our relationship with God, his writings (like those of Teresa) contain powerful insights into the dynamics of any relationship that seeks consummation in a union of mind, body, and heart.

As John describes it, people who have given themselves over to God and have enjoyed a rich prayer life, imbued with a sense of God's presence and bearing fruit in good works, are sure to be challenged by a period of time when God seems to be absent, when prayer seems to be empty and hypocritical, and when good works are performed mechanically, if at all.

John assures his readers that this dark night is something to rejoice in. It is a sign that the soul's relationship with God has proceeded to a point where God begins to prepare the soul for lasting union with God. With God's immediate presence withdrawn, the soul is forced to get down to brass tacks. Is devotion to God dependent on spiritual comfort, or is it grounded in religious and moral principles that transcend personal happiness? John raises the stakes even higher. If God does not seem to exist, will the soul be faithful to God anyway? Having been set on fire by the apprehension of a loving will at the heart of everything, will the soul continue to cast its lot on the side of sacrificial self-giving, even if it appears that there is no God to model such love or to underwrite it?

As the soul struggles with these questions, it becomes aware of how much its own self-centeredness continues to hold sway. It is challenged to yield itself to God once again, with no thought of reward and with no certainty that God is there to receive the gift. So the soul, which has been stripped of all its props, voluntarily advances further into the dark night, casting off its needs and demands as it goes, and resting in nothing but its pure love for God. What John is describing, of course, is unilateral love. In the dark night, the soul is given the opportunity to love God in this way. Without such a pure self-offering, devoid of any hope or expectation of reward, true union with God is not possible. Why? Because God's love is also unilateral: it is self-initiated and expects nothing in return. True union with God is the union of two such loves.

So what about a union between two human beings? If, as I have argued, a lifelong union schools us for union with every neighbor and with God, then it should not surprise us if something like the dark night of the soul assails every faithful lover at some point along the way. If the ultimate purpose of the union is to school us in radical self-giving love, then a couple that settles for comfort and familiarity has fallen short of its original goal. A dark night remains, in which each party must examine what private fantasy, what personal bitterness, what unforgiven hurt stands in the way of total devotion to the beloved. Unlike the dark night that assails the soul in its relationship with God, there is no question of the beloved's existence and presence. But I may still wonder if my partner is still (or ever was) the person I thought I was uniting myself to. The answer is probably no. It's not just that my partner has developed and changed over time. It's likely that I never truly saw my partner in the first place. If the analogy to the dark night holds, there are false projections to be stripped away, not only so that the lover can rediscover the beloved as originally envisioned and loved, but so that the original vision can be clarified and cleansed of all false overlays.

Overcoming Ambivalence

As I mentioned, if and when the dark night comes, refusing to undergo it can hurt the other partner. How can this be avoided? Throughout this chapter, we have been considering how hurtful behavior in relationships is directly related to ambivalence about those relationships. So resolving the ambivalence should result in lessening the hurt. I have also argued that ambivalence has to do with fear of commitment and resistance to truth-telling. If I am correct in suggesting that achieving the deepest and truest union involves something like the dark night of the soul, then this fear and this resistance must be wrestled to the ground and conquered before true union between partner and partner can be attained. This struggle, which comes to no two persons in exactly the same way or form, is first and foremost a spiritual struggle. Like Jacob wrestling with the angel, we must fight with God who demands that we give ourselves over in trust, and that we love truth more than comfort.

But embracing the dark night is also about submitting to the beloved. In part this means placing myself in my beloved's hands—thus putting my complete trust in someone other than myself. That is scary enough. But it also means placing myself under another's authority, which is perhaps even scarier. In general, we should be suspicious of any demand to forego our autonomy, even if we seem to encounter such a demand in the Bible. Parallel passages in Ephesians and Colossians (Ephesians 5:22–24; 6:5–8); Colossians 3:18; 3:22–25) command wives to submit to their husbands and slaves to submit to their masters. Such passages cannot be taken at face value, but must be approached critically, in light of the social context in which they were originally written, but also in light of the impulse toward spiritual freedom and radical equality that characterizes the early Christian witness as a whole. That impulse is itself grounded in these believers' submission to Christ and his submission, in turn, to the will of the One who sent him. This is not as paradoxical as it sounds. If God is love, then subordinating our wills to God's is the same thing as receiving the capacity to love as God loves, and so becoming free. This is the submission we profess every time we say the prayer Jesus taught us to pray: "Thy kingdom come; thy will be done on earth as it is in heaven." It is the submission Jesus himself makes just moments before his arrest: "Father, if you are willing, remove this cup from me; yet not my will but yours be done" (Luke 22:42). But doesn't the meaning of submission shift the moment we apply it to our relationship with God? The emphasis is not so much on subordination as on *joining* ourselves to God, so that God's cause is our cause and God's work our work. There is real danger involved in this, as the cross of Christ reminds us daily. To be drawn into the force field of the divine love is to feel keenly all that stands against that love, whether it assaults us from outside or rises up within us as the residue of our own hard-heartedness. But this is not a danger that God poses—God wants nothing but our good. It is the danger posed by all that resists the love of God.

If submission to God is not essentially about hierarchy, neither then is submission to one's life-partner about who's the "boss." It must have to do with our discernment of the beloved's relationship with God, and the commitment we make to support that relationship and to be guided by it. It is a commonplace to speak of the face of Christ in the face of the neighbor. In one sense, every person is Christ to me, since Jesus identifies himself with everyone, especially the most abject (Matthew 25:31–46). But we may also understand this in another way. We see the face of Christ in the face of another person who models Jesus' submission to the Father's will, and so elicits from us a devotion and loyalty analogous to our submission to Christ. The goal of a life-partnership is to know one's partner so well that one sees clearly where God has taken hold, where the heart has been joined to God. My goal is to discern where my beloved has become like Christ, and to give myself over to that.

But this brings us back to the dark night. In the first dawning of true love, we are bowled over by the spiritual beauty of the beloved.

We see that beauty far more clearly than he or she can. But there may come times when failure, disappointment and loss take the beloved into a terrible place where we cannot follow, or take us into a darkness that makes it difficult for us to be in touch with our beloved. Here nothing avails but faith in what cannot be seen. All that can be seen and known is our initial promise to remain in the relationship for life, and our memory of the discernment and vision that elicited that promise in the first place. To be reduced to mere obedience—"I will keep my promise, I will stay with you, not because I feel like it or because it makes sense to me, but because I am obligated to do so"—is to stand at the threshold of a more perfect union. In part, the dark night forces us to remember that our partner is also our neighbor—since we don't have much to go on besides that. But it also clarifies the union, boiling it down to its essential element: the gift of oneself, freely given, with no strings attached.

1. How do you deal with conflict as a couple? Do you have explosive screaming matches? Do you give each other "the silent treatment"? How do you perceive your partner as dealing with conflict?

2. How does your partner tell you "truths" in your relationship? How do you deal with these truths? In what ways are you able to talk about them? If you do not talk about them, why don't you?

3. Are you giving yourself to your partner with no strings attached? Have you truly put aside all of the temptations and fears that are part of the human condition that cloud your relationship? (Keep in mind, this is not a question only for those about to embark on this journey; this question may be addressed at any point in the journey of a sacred union.)

Exercise:

Choose one (or more) of the three areas of ambivalence outlined in the chapter—fear, truth-telling, or self-giving—to examine within yourself. Don't be afraid to look deep within yourself for the source of whatever brings any doubt into your relationship with your partner. If you are comfortable, write these things out on paper; then decide what you are able to share with your beloved. Share as much as feels possible in an effort to work out between you your ambivalence. This is hard work, but doing it now will give you tools for dealing with difficult situations further down the road.

EIGHT

Consummation

So far we have been focusing on the challenges and disciplines of sacred union. But now we are ready to consider the happiness that is inherent in this way of life. That happiness lies in the peculiar kind of fellowship sacred union bestows on those who enter into it. This is a fellowship grounded in closeness and transcendence, perfect equality and total submission. This total conjunction of familiarity and mystery, which is the unique signature of sacred union, results directly from the fact that the lover's sexual passion has been so suffused with charity—the love of God and of the neighbor in God—that the one cannot be distinguished from the other. To borrow Luther's arresting image for the way the soul is transformed by faith, the charity that charges the lover's sexual desire is like the heat that turns a piece of cold iron into white-hot metal.[11] When this conversion occurs, the companionship both partners enjoy becomes an invitation into divine grace, such that the love they share truly incarnates God's love for them and all of humankind.

Encountering the Kingdom of God

We began this discussion by suggesting that a sacred union ultimately looks beyond itself to the reign of God, where we experience union with everyone. But as with all practices that anticipate the reign of God, a lifelong union is also an end in itself. Like the Eucharist, it is not just a stepping-stone on the way to something better—it is a first encounter with life in the kingdom. The post-communion prayer we use at the Princeton University Chapel puts it well: "We thank you for beginning in us the age that is to come." So, while forming a union and establishing a household are not easy tasks, they also bring their own internal rewards. Life in a union makes possible a degree and quality of companionship over time that cannot be matched anywhere else in this world. This is due in part to the sexual dimension of the relationship, in part to the assumption that under normal circumstances the partners will not be separated for long periods of time, and in part to the fact that the couple possesses everything in common.

We would not expect to find any of these factors in the best of friendships—even one of them would make it look more like a union than a friendship. The relationship of parents to children and siblings to siblings comes close to affording a similar level of connection and fellowship, but quite apart from the imperative that sex be categorically excluded from these relationships, no one would ever assume that children should live out their adult lives under the same roof as their parents. As I noted in chapter six, parenting includes equipping children eventually to leave home.

The closest analogue to sacred union is probably a contemporary monastic community. Monks and nuns forego sexual relations altogether, but they pursue a common life in which all goods are shared. In many instances they also make a commitment to remain in the same community for life. Certainly, the monastic life demands and makes possible a level of fellowship and mutual devotion equaling that of a sacred union. In fact, some monks and nuns internally refer to their commitment to the community as marriage, wearing a wedding ring as a symbol of their commitment to the community and to God.

But there is an important difference here, connected but not reducible to the fact that sexual relations—including monogamous ones—are typically prohibited in monasticism. In most traditions, monks and nuns are not supposed to form special attachments to other community members. In part this helps to keep each individual's focus on God. But avoiding any personal dynamic that approaches romance also ensures that the fellowship enjoyed in the monastic house is as inclusive and communal as possible. Thus, what is lost in intimacy is gained in available time for devotional practices and personal availability to as many brothers or sisters as possible.

The contrast with lifelong unions is illuminating. Both monasticism and union provide the opportunity to get ready for life with countless neighbors in God's kingdom. But when two partners form a union, they are focusing all of their rehearsal time on each other. The result is not so much a diminished focus on God and community as a compression of the singular figure of the beloved. The devotion of each partner is so concentrated on the other that the other's face becomes the face of every neighbor and the face of God. I don't mean that the particular identity of the beloved gets taken up into a larger category, or that the beloved becomes an object of worship instead of God. I mean that true love confers on the beloved the same extravagant devotion that every neighbor could expect from us if we had more love to go around.

The consequence of this intense devotion to one person is that we can begin to imagine how differently we might perceive others if they were the objects of a comparable devotion. Once this connection is made, everything I learn about how to be a good lover to my partner (or how to avoid being a bad lover) becomes an object lesson for my schooling in neighbor-love. If my partner becomes chronically ill and all my time away from work is given over to home care, I am being changed into someone more willing to serve at the bedside of strangers. If I choose to stand by my partner who has been—justly or unjustly—brought to shame, then I am volunteering to become someone who stands in solidarity with the poor and with all who are despised. If I really hear my partner telling me that I am too quick to find fault or to disparage, I will perhaps be ready to see how a tendency to put others down poisons all my relationships.

I will tell a story on myself. After our wedding, Margaret and I moved immediately to Oxford, where we lived for two years. Margaret kidded me that I had adopted the hint of an English accent during the year of our engagement, when I was living alone in Oxford and she was still in the States. She was right—I had. Partly I wanted not to stick out as an American; partly I was enjoying the chance to try on a different persona. Margaret understood all this, and was kindly about it, if amused. But she was not amused when, one day, a few weeks into our life in England, I asked her to be quiet. We were walking across Tom Quad—the large front quadrangle of Christ Church, my college—when we spotted a Canadian friend rounding the corner on the other side. Margaret shouted a greeting, and the two began a conversation across the open expanse of the quad. This is when I asked Margaret to keep her voice down. "What did you say?" she asked, her voice tight with anger. As soon as we were alone, she let me have it: "Don't you ever tell me to be quiet." As we worked through this painful episode, I realized I had not wanted Margaret to blow my cover. I didn't want people to realize I was an American, so I didn't want her drawing attention to her unashamedly American voice. This was a huge lesson for me. It compelled me to question (not for the first time, I might add) my own dissatisfaction with my own identity, but also to examine my propensity to make anyone associated with me project a certain image. This remains a challenge for me, and probably always will. For instance, I have to be very careful that I do not try to orchestrate worship in the Princeton University Chapel so that it gives the "right" impression of my own liturgical preferences. It's not that chapel worship doesn't reflect on me—of course it does, because I am so closely connected with it. The point is that I can never control what reflects on me, nor should I forget that who I really am is also not within my control—my identity has been shaped as much by others as by me, and continues to be reshaped and refreshed in their hands. This seems obvious to me now, but I might still be blind to this if Margaret had not refused early on to put up with being silenced.

Sometimes such lessons are learned in bed. The things we learn about ourselves when we are having sex tell us a lot about what we can expect from each other at the dinner table or in parent-teacher conferences. They also tell us a lot about our dealings with other people generally. If I do not wholeheartedly give myself sexually to my partner, this is a sure indication that I am also unavailable in all kinds of ways to my children, my parents, my colleagues and clients, and my God. It does not matter that, unlike all these other relationships, my relationship to my partner is sexual. Precisely because sex exposes us so dramatically to the beloved as neighbor, how we negotiate that exposure reveals a great deal about where we stand in regard to relationships in general. At the same time, what we struggle with and work through in our sexual relationship to our partner is immediately applicable to all our other relationships, including our relationship with God. Again: the face of the beloved is also the face of the neighbor and the face of God.

Sacred Unions and Neighbor-Love

So we know this much: The blessing afforded by sacred union cannot be explained or experienced without reference to the sacred union's fundamental connection with neighbor-love. Whatever happiness we can expect to garner through a lifetime of fidelity to one person hinges on our capacity to love the beloved selflessly and without thought of reward. This is a tall order. It is relatively easy to project neighbor-love onto those who are far off or only intermittently present; it is entirely another matter to love one's own partner and one's household in the same way.

As we saw in chapter seven, how we treat each other at close range reveals the true measure of our progress toward genuine love of neighbor. Most of us still have a long way to go. Falling in love is only the beginning of the process whereby each partner is fully schooled in true love. The dark night we talked about is the turning point in this process. There comes a point in each partner's journey toward an ever deeper and more mature union when desire for the other must be cleansed of whatever self-centeredness remains. Since love of God and love of the neighbor are so tightly linked, these two dark nights are closely related as well, and the spiritual struggle entailed in each is in reality the same struggle. In chapter seven we only considered this struggle as something likely to be resisted; we did not discuss what it is like to come out on the other side. But it's important that we think this through: if we understand what is going on in that dark time, we will also understand where we are ultimately headed when we enter into a lifelong union.

Coming Out of the Darkness

I return here to Spenser's *Faerie Queene,* which so brilliantly maps out the landscape of true love. Book 1 of this epic poem is about holiness, and it is not surprising that Spenser chooses to explore the path to sanctity by telling the story of England's patron saint, George, and his slaying of the dragon. What might be less expected is that Spenser frames this tale of sanctification as a love story about the knight (known throughout most of the book as "the Redcross knight" because of the red cross emblazoned on his shield) and his beloved, the beautiful Una, who seeks his help to rescue her homeland from the dragon's ravages. At one level the poem is about how an ordinary person gains the grace to become a Christlike vanquisher of evil. But the poem can also be read as the story of a young man who is learning what true love is all about. These two levels of interpretation can share one story line because, as Spenser well knew, romance is itself about sanctification.

The dark night begins for Redcross when he falls into conversation with Despair, a character who enumerates the knight's misdeeds, argues that it is unlikely that he could ever be saved, and offers him a noose with which to hang himself (*Faerie Queene* 1:9:33–34). I say this is the dark night because Redcross is being made to face his own past. But it is important to note that for Spenser, despair itself is a way to avoid the dark night. Redcross's submission to despair caps all his other sins put together. The knight is willing to take his life rather than live with the knowledge of his own failure and move forward with the grace of God. So in a sense the dark night has *not* yet arrived, because Redcross is still running from it.

> Spenser's Una is a complex figure. At the most basic level, she is a young woman in love with Redcross, as well as a devoted daughter who has sought out this young knight's help to rescue her parents from the ravages of a terrible dragon. But Una is many other things as well. Her name means "One," and in her character she embodies the Church in its essential unity of fellowship and faith ("There is one Body and one Spirit, one hope in God's call to us; one Lord, one Faith, one Baptism; one God and Father of all"). As such, she is no damsel in distress, but a powerful instrument of divine grace who calls Redcross to account for his faithlessness and oversees the painful schooling that finally makes him fit to play the hero's part.

It is only when Una arrives on the scene, fiercely upbraids Redcross, and leads him to the House of Holiness for a severe regime of penitence and healing, that he begins to own the consequences of his pride and move forward. The key to this episode is Redcross's rescue by Una, and his acquiescence in this rescue. By all accounts, one would say that Redcross hits bottom when he falls into the hands of Despair. It is at this point, after all, that the knight realizes the extent to which he has failed to be a Christlike savior for Una. But the real nadir comes when Redcross must—and does—accept salvation at Una's hands. She is Christ for him, although he has botched every opportunity so far to be Christ for her. This is the final humiliation.

We will fail to see what is really happening here if we interpret Redcross's humiliation in terms of gender roles. Redcross has not failed as a man; in his view he has failed as a lover. Remember that the whole Christian romantic tradition hinges on the troubadours' identification of faithful sexual love with Christ's self-sacrificing love. From his or her own point of view, the lover is always called to play this role, and the beloved is viewed as deigning (or not) to return that love. But the beloved, from her own perspective, perceives herself as Christ also. Una does not seem to think that she is undergoing a role reversal when she rescues Redcross. She is exhibiting the same care, and exercising the same kind of authority, that she has exhibited in earlier episodes. The difference between Una and Redcross is that she moves easily back and forth between rescuing and being rescued, while it is shameful to Redcross that he should be in a position where he cannot protect Una, let alone save himself. Yet until he acknowledges his complete dependence on her (and by implication his gratitude that she has saved his life), he cannot begin the process of healing that eventually fits him to play Christ's part against the dragon.

Rescued by True Love

The theological message here is clear. Spenser is reminding us that salvation is by faith, not works. Our own efforts get us nowhere; God's unmerited but abundant grace gets us everywhere. The Redcross Knight becomes Saint George the moment he owns his failings without despairing, and places all his trust in God. The message regarding romance is clear, too. We cannot fully give ourselves to another in true love until we are willing to receive the love of the beloved, not as a love returned but as unmerited grace. This is a message the romantic tradition needs to hear over and over. A tradition born out of the identification of the true lover with

Christ has to keep learning that no one can imitate Christ who has not first been rescued by him. None of us can bypass the narrow door of spiritual destitution. This means that as a lover I cannot always play Jesus. I must let my beloved be Jesus to me. It's not enough that I acknowledge my failings as a lover. I must be willing to admit how needy I am of rescue by my partner.

The rescue I most need is the refuge of love. But this love is very different from the love I might have expected before I entered the dark night. In its initial boldness, romantic love expects (or hopes) that the love it offers will be reciprocated, and this despite the fact that it understands its own offering of love to be unilateral: the initiative lies solely with each lover. But true love is not complete until it understands that the beloved's love is *also* unilateral. I am not loved back because I have done the heroic thing and loved first. I am passive in the face of the other's initiative, more dependent, more needy than I could ever have admitted. But to come to this realization and to embrace it is finally to be possessed of a love that is clean. In the mystical dark night, this is the point at which the soul, having emptied itself of all its pride and pretension, becomes fully possessed by God. Similarly, the lover who yields himself entirely into the hands of the beloved for the first time lets her all the way into his life. This is the moment when the lover's desire for the beloved is transformed into charity, that love of God and neighbor that is best described as the movement of the whole person toward the other in thanksgiving. This *eucharistic* act—a word that literally means "thanksgiving"—has nothing to do with reciprocation; it belongs to an entirely different economy.

Just as the gifts of bread and wine offered up in the Eucharist already belong to God, and it is God's own Spirit that moves within us in our act of offering, the true lover knows well that his rapture is itself the gift and grace of the beloved who has made him her own. And just as those who take the Eucharist (Holy Communion) receive the grace to take up Christ's ministry in the world, so the lover who has put aside his pretensions about being

Christ to the beloved is also now enabled to serve his beloved with pure affection.

Equality and Submission

The yielding I have attempted to describe here is the consummation of sacred union. I have presented it as a singular event, but in fact it is a complex process of transformation that may stretch over years and may need at some point to be repeated. Anyone who has experienced this yielding knows the joy of it and knows it to be both the purpose of sacred union and its fulfillment. Once both partners are willing to be receivers who cannot pay back, as well as givers who expect no return, the union comes into its own as a spiritual dynamic in which equality and submission both play a part. Each is equally a giver and a receiver; by turns, each wields the authority of Christ or yields to it.

This constant exchange resolves a fundamental tension at the heart of human affairs, namely, how to honor the principle of human equality without failing to acknowledge the dimension of authority and submission in the relationship of neighbor to neighbor. The back-and-forth movement of authority and initiative from one partner to the other has always been the secret of a successful union, although this has been masked both by the hierarchical model long associated with traditional marriage, as well as by the model of autonomy associated with "modern" relationships. Neither model does justice to this dynamic.

The model of autonomy highlights the equal dignity we have as children of God, made in God's image. The hierarchical highlights the authority we have over each other, in our right to each other's attention and care, and in our capacity to see other people better than they can see themselves. Taken alone, each model distorts and limits human relationships. Because it does not take equality sufficiently into account, the hierarchical model freezes the dynamics of authority in a single moment, ignoring the movement of authority from person to person. Because the model of autonomy leaves authority out of account, it offers no explanation for the way we really are related to each other through the giving and receiving, the speaking and listening, in which we alternately exercise authority and submit to it. As I hope I have shown, the romantic model brings initiative and authority into proper relationship, and accounts for the interplay of freedom and submission, which is the distinguishing feature of sacred union.

But as I also hope I have shown, every sacred union is continually a work in progress. When a couple exchanges vows of lifelong fidelity, shared fortune, and unqualified mutual respect, they create a union that is sacred by anticipation. The initiative each partner takes in making this vow is not in most cases the truly Christlike act it will become once each partner has tasted the dark night. But if each partner endures that purification with humility and trust, and if the other is attentive and patient, then the holiness we hope for will be realized, as each one takes up the cross of Christ, and with it Christ's joy.

1. What are the joys of your relationship? What is it about your partner that causes you a feeling of ecstasy that cannot be duplicated in any other way?

2. How will you approach the time in your relationship when your partner is experiencing the dark night? What steps can you take now to prepare yourself and your relationship for the inevitable growth that will happen as you are together?

3. Who are you? As an individual? As a member of this sacred union? Where are the points of dissonance between your sense of self and your part in this union? Where are the points of harmony? How can you take steps both alone and with your partner to strengthen the harmony?

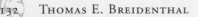

Exercise:

Together, watch the film *The Princess Bride*. Although this is, on the surface, a comedy, on a deeper level, it is a quintessential story of true love, and the power it holds when it is pure. Pay close attention to the relationship between Wesley and Buttercup. See how they go through the dark night of separation (both physical and psychological) and even death. While this is fantasy, and Miracle Max conquers death instead of God, it is symbolic of the power true love can hold upon all our lives. Take what you can from this contemporary fairy tale and apply it to your own relationship.

Loss

THERE ARE SPIRITUAL PATHS WITHIN CHRISTIANITY AND outside of it that are centered on detachment from material goods as well as from personal relationships, but lifelong union is not one of them. True love is all about attachment. Those who enter into this path attach themselves to each other as intentionally as they can, and this attachment only deepens and grows stronger over time. So what do we do when the other is torn away, whether by death, illness, or breakdown of the relationship?

I have not experienced the loss of a partner, but I do know what it feels like to fear such a loss. So I will start by talking about that fear and the various forms it takes. I have a hunch that the way we live into that fear has a lot to do with how we handle loss when it comes our way, as it inevitably will.

Fear of Loss

Young lovers preparing to enter into a lifelong union are more likely to be afraid of failure than of death. This is a realistic fear, given the high divorce rate. When I look back on the year of our engagement, I realize I was more anxious about this than I cared to acknowledge at the time. I especially recall one incident. The day of the ceremony was fast approaching, and since it was going to take place in the parish church where I had served as an assistant, the whole thing had taken on a life of its own, with more and more of the congregation getting involved one way or another. The rector—my former boss—had been providing our premarital counseling. It was our last session, and he was joking about how much energy was being focused on this particular exchange of vows. Suddenly, he leaned across his desk, fixed me with a steady gaze, and said, not jokingly, "We're not doing this again. This had better stick."

Fear of failure is natural, particularly when the outcome matters to so many people, as is always the case with a sacred union. But unless that fear has been ignited by something specific—a worrisome pattern of behavior on the other's part, or the realization that one is not in love after all—it's not worth acting on. The genuine desire to spend your life with a person you are attracted to in body, mind, and heart is like faith in God. We no more choose to love that person than we choose to believe in God. Nor can we achieve more certainty about the genuineness and permanence of our love than we can about the genuineness and permanence of our faith. Yet it would be absurd to reject faith lest we should lose it in the future. So it is with true love. It befalls us, and we can hardly refuse it because it might go sour down the line. If our love is genuine, we must simply give ourselves over to it, and tomorrow will take care of itself.

Faith and Doubt

That is not to say that genuine love is free from doubt. Here again, romantic love is like faith in God. They both attract doubt the way fruit attracts flies. Why? Because they both rest in convictions that cannot be proven. Faith places us in the hands of a God we cannot see, still less get our minds around. Love arises within us unbidden, and for all our love letters and poems, is never able to give an adequate reason why it finds its object and satisfaction in this person and not some other. So both faith and love are open to question, and should be. We are thinking beings, and it is right that we should question anything that seems to be beyond proof, if only to make certain that what we are calling our love or our faith is not an easy cover for something else we resist looking at squarely.

In this sense, doubt is the servant of truth. So doubt may well question my faith in God by asking if I am simply projecting my own need for protection and control onto a higher power. In that case, it would be better to forget about God and address my need for protection and control. But it often turns out that doubt provokes me to examine the genuineness of my faith. It may turn out, on examination, that, far from seeking protection and control, I am willing to forego all kinds of safety and predictability for the sake of engagement with a God whom I perceive to be pressing in upon me on all sides, and whom I long to know.

And so it is with love. We question ourselves individually and as couples, to ensure that our devotion is neither self-serving nor self-destroying. The chief purpose of premarital counseling is to bring forward and articulate the questions that anyone intending to create a union is bound to be asking anyway. If truth be told, the usual questions—about money, religion, and service—as challenging as these may be in their own right, are really meant to be catalysts for far deeper questions: "How much are you really willing to give up for each other? Can you trust each other to be faithful? Do you delight in each other's company?" It is a skillful pastor who can help a couple raise these questions in their own way and, one hopes, be strengthened in the conviction that their love is true.

In any case, doubt is seldom in itself a sign of trouble. It is in the nature of love to inspire doubt. If love is willing to be assailed by doubt, and can stand up to it robustly, then it is probably genuine, and all concerned should support it and rejoice in it.

Jealousy

There is one form of fear, however, that does spell trouble. That is jealousy. Sometimes jealousy is not a bad thing, if it is simply the reasonable desire not to be stepped out on. If you have forsworn all other sexual relations in favor of a union with your partner, you may well get your guard up if there appears to be another person in the picture, to say nothing of the anger you will feel if you discover that your partner's vow of fidelity has been broken. This is the kind of jealousy God exhibits for the children of Israel in the Hebrew Scriptures, and which Jesus exhibits in all four Gospels when he cleanses the Temple: "Zeal (that is, jealousy) for your house has eaten me up," comments John, quoting Psalm 69 (see John 2:17).

But there is another kind of jealousy that is not reasonable, because it falsely claims that the right not to be stepped out on implies the right to prevent one's partner from having any other significant relationships. The reason for wanting to make my right over my partner absolute is the fear that any other relationship, even that of parent to child, threatens my own relationship to my partner. The only way a nonsexual relationship could threaten the primary bond uniting partner to partner would be if that bond precluded all kinds of significant connections with the rest of the human race. But to view that bond in this way flies in the face of everything that has been said so far about sacred unions. The purpose of sacred unions is to equip us for more connection to other people, not less. Sexual fidelity to a single partner allows us to practice the disciplines of neighbor-love in a framework that is manageable and relatively safe, but it by no means precludes the application of those disciplines over a wide range of friendships, peer relations, and constant encounters with strangers. Jealousy that seeks to prevent the partner from enjoying that wide range of connections is a distortion of true love.

Anyone given to lifelong partnership is susceptible to this distortion, and needs to steer clear of it. Attachment to one's partner can easily turn into a desire to possess him exclusively. It is easy not to notice this shift from attachment to possessiveness, because in its first stages it goes hand in hand with a devotion to the beloved that is ready to grant whatever the beloved wants, including friendships and personal responsibilities outside of the primary relationship.

Such devotion can easily turn into annexation. This is especially true if we lose sight of the fact that true love, as the Christian romantic tradition understands it, has nothing to do with gaining control over the beloved. It's just the opposite. What makes the beloved seem godlike is that, as my neighbor and a child of God, she is completely out of my control. She has a destiny that I cannot interfere with. This insight lies at the heart of the troubadour tradition. When that insight is replaced by a fixed desire to latch my beloved into an orbit that has me as its center, we are no longer dealing with love but idolatry.

From the biblical point of view, idolatry is not simply a matter of misdirected worship. It is a matter of attempting to find something worthy of worship that, unlike God, we can control. As we have seen, the romantic tradition celebrates the fact that the human object of our devotion can be a window onto God and the neighbor. Celebrating this runs the risk of idolatry rather than devotion, since what looks like devotion may be emotional greed masquerading as love. The risk is worth it, however, because a lifetime of faithful partnership is such a powerful training ground for love of God and neighbor. But if I discern within myself a drift toward jealousy, I should address it right away.

So far we have been considering the fear of failure—fear of mutual incompatibility, or of untrustworthiness on the partner's part. But sometimes the expectation of a harmonious and joyous life with the love of our life can cause us to be afraid.

Making Fear Your Friend

All too many of us grow up believing that we don't deserve to be happy. So when we encounter the possibility of happiness in love, we assume it cannot last. I had not been at seminary long when, during the course of a visit back to my home parish, I had occasion to spend some time with Louise, one of the friends I had made there through the Episcopal chaplaincy on campus. Eventually the conversation turned to her personal life. Louise told me she had found the person she wanted to spend the rest of her life with, and that they were talking about marriage. All of a sudden she began to cry. She said she was so afraid that something would happen to take them away from each other.

I don't know how helpful I was at the time—I had not yet found my heart's desire—but I know what I would say to someone in a similar situation today. To find true love is God's own gift to us. God does not play games with us. God will not give us happiness to lure us into a false hope of God's love for us. God may have challenges in store for us that we could not have met without this taste of happiness, and those challenges may include the loss of our partner. But God is steadfast. God does not give with one hand and take away with another. As Paul reminds us: "The Son of God . . . was not 'Yes and No;' but in him it is always 'Yes.' For in him every one of God's promises is a 'Yes'" (1 Corinthians 1:19–20).

At the same time we should not disregard our fear, because fear casts our priorities into high relief. Furthermore, when we see that our fear of loss is proportional to the seriousness of our love, the fear becomes less debilitating. Not long after my conversation with Louise, I was back at seminary preparing for crucial meetings in my home diocese—meetings that would determine whether or not I would be permitted to move forward to ordination. Such meetings are standard, but every seminarian dreads them. It doesn't matter how many assurances you receive that everything will be fine, it is perfectly clear that it is possible to fail. A few days before my flight home, I was walking from class toward my dormitory when I was seized with panic. I was sure that I would not be approved for ordination, and I could not imagine what I would do with my life if that happened. In that very moment, as if it was coming to me from outside myself, I heard a voice say, "Make the fear your friend."

I won't try here to explore all the ways in which that suggestion or command has spoken to me over the years. Fundamentally, it has taught me that fear is always the flip side of vocation. Whatever we feel called to and identified by will present itself to us as something we could not bear to lose. Fear and attachment go together. But if we acknowledge the attachment whose loss we dread, we gain a certain peace. This is what I am all about, and this constitutes the particular set of people, jobs, and things I would find it catastrophic to do without. To give our hearts to anyone or anything is to define where our future suffering will be located. For me, making fear my friend has meant letting my fear show me what is most precious to me, and owning my fear as an expression of my love.

Preparing for Loss by Loving Our Neighbors

But how are those of us living our lives in sacred unions to prepare ourselves for the day when loss is not merely something feared but a reality? This is something of a riddle. As I suggested at the beginning of this chapter, sacred union is all about attachment. How can a way of life that is so centered in attachment train us for the forcible detachment that comes when a partner dies, or is imprisoned, or becomes inaccessible through illness?

The answer lies, I think, in the fact that our passionate focus on one partner is constantly training us to be more available to every neighbor who comes our way. The more we give our lives over to serving the needs of a partner who is in trouble or sick or dying, the more ready we will be, once our grief abates somewhat, to engage a whole host of neighbors in ways we could not have imagined earlier. Conversely, engaging the suffering of neighbors other than our partner aids us in understanding loss at a less emotionally volatile level, and thus may prepare us for the time when it is our closest neighbor—our partner—who is in need of our service.

It is easy to forget that sacred unions are essentially provisional, even though we enter into them for life. The traditional vows by which Christians have bound themselves to each other for life end with a clause about death: the vow extends only "until death us do part." Christianity has always avoided the notion of a marriage bond extending beyond the grave. Why? At the most practical level, the Christian community recognizes the need for widow and widower to find solace in life with a new partner. At a deeper level, this teaching goes well beyond the vicissitudes of this life and spells out how true love anticipates our relationship with every neighbor in the kingdom of God.

My bond with my wife does not preclude bonds with every other neighbor—instead, it is a preparation for them. It is precisely through my attachment to my partner, not in spite of it, that I give myself over more and more to the world. If the time comes when I am alone again, I should find myself more open to the neighbor, closer to God, and clearer about who I am than I was before my partner and I first came together.

I don't mean that the partnership is itself just another place in which I encounter the world in all its overwhelming challenge and ambiguity. I regard my family as a refuge from all that. (Of course, household life presents its own challenges and ambiguities, but that's not what I mean here.) When all is said and done, the disciplines and practices we have talked about in this book relate to the creation and preservation of a refuge from which we emerge more equipped to engage the world, not less. Why? It is because the household provides us with a relatively safe space to love and to be loved without reservation, and so it is there that we experience the power of the cross firsthand.

But even as I am taking refuge in my partner, I am—or should be—sharing in her friendships, getting to know the new people she brings into my life. From the first tentative visits with a lover's parents and the informal interviews with a best friend to see if you pass muster, to the holiday lunch with a spouse's office mates, the union draws each partner into an expanding circle of fellowship, very often with very different people. When one partner dies, his closest friends outside the union can be a major element of support for the partner who has been left behind, and can provide the best opportunity for him to begin venturing out into the world as a single person. Many saw this happen over and over again during the AIDS epidemic, and this pattern of reaching out is familiar to anyone who has spent much time in any church congregation. It is as if we knew instinctively that our connection with the deceased helps the grieving partner to embrace life among others for the lost partner's sake.

So my partner, who is for me the quintessential neighbor, who provides my gateway into a whole network of well-wishers I might not otherwise have had, and who functions as a placeholder for countless others whom I do not know or am not ready for, keeps me in practice for neighbor-love in the wide world. But that is not all my partner does to prepare me for eventual loss. I spoke earlier of the prophetic role the partner can play, revealing aspects of our character of which we were unaware, and calling us back to our spiritual journey when we begin to lose our way. By teaching me about myself and calling me to be all that I can be, my partner prepares me to face life alone as a self who is self-aware. Of course, to lose this prophetic voice is to lose the incomparable blessing of a conversation partner who is on my side. A pastor or therapist can provide this kind of support, and such professional help should always be sought, if necessary. But when it comes to having a sounding board that is available at any hour of the day or night, and a critical observer who knows us inside and out, nothing can make up for a life partner. Pastors and therapists may know us for years, may care for us deeply, and can offer absolution and good advice, but only a life partner confirms this with his or her own daily presence, in bed, at the dinner table, in a reassuring email from the office.

"What I miss the most . . ."

This highlights another way in which loss can be devastating. A colleague who lost her husband to cancer a few years ago—they had fallen in love in high school—tells me that what she misses most is his wisdom and perspective on things, so different from her own. Another friend whose partner died suddenly at the age of forty says he simply did not realize how much he depended on him for even the simplest decision. This is completely understandable. In my own marriage, I depend so heavily on Margaret's insight that life without that extra pair of eyes is unthinkable. The very intensity of our exchanges helps me be clearer about my vocation, my spiritual goals, and the ways in which I stand in the way of God's grace. It has gotten to the point that, if I want Margaret's take on something and she is not around to offer it, I can hear her voice in my own head and be pretty sure what she would say. (Not that my imagining what Margaret would say is a substitute for the real thing—her analysis of a situation can still contain surprises.) Not only do I depend on her being there when I come seeking advice. I also count on her to let me know when I am behaving foolishly or irresponsibly. More often than not, those comments are unsolicited, but much needed!

What this means, of course, is that her perspective has enriched my own. I cannot say that I see things through her eyes, because her place in God's world will always be different from my own. But what I have learned from her over many years of life together has become a part of my own outlook. In the same way, Margaret's sense of who I am has changed me. Some false expectations have fallen away; some new expectations have emerged. I am not only a different person from the one I was when we married, but, and perhaps more importantly, I have a surer knowledge of myself. This means that, whatever the future holds, I will meet it with the resources Margaret has helped to forge.

Reclaiming Life After Loss

To be clear: I don't mean that our relationship with God and our self-identity is so bound up with our life partner that we have no path to either except through our partner, whether in conversation or through memory. I have known people whose loss has been so spiritually disorienting that any attention to their partner's impact on them has only led to more devastation and disorientation. Sometimes what is needed is to locate a place in oneself that is not bound up with the union. A man once told me this story. His wife had suddenly and unexpectedly died of heart failure, shortly after both of them had retired. Although he tried to put a brave face on it, his grief was overwhelming. He could hardly bear to continue living in his house, where he was reminded of her everywhere he turned, and he managed to be out of town while his sons sorted through his wife's effects.

One day he took it into his mind to revisit a formative experience that occurred before he ever met his wife. When he was a young man in southern Oregon, his work required him to shuttle back and forth between Ashland—on one side of the Cascade range— and Klamath Falls—on the other. This is a back road, not much traveled. On one of these trips east, in the summertime, around midnight, under the light of a full moon, and with the highway to himself, he turned off his headlights. He had cleared the divide and was headed down the long eastern slope, with the road straight before him and the vast forest of ponderosas and cedars rising up on both sides. With his windows down in the old Ford he could hear the wind in the treetops. Sometimes he stopped the engine and listened to the sounds of the forest all around him. It took him all night, but he never regretted it.

Now, as an old man afflicted by grief, he decided to drive the old road to Klamath Falls and to turn off the lights again. He waited for the full moon and set off in his Saab at about ten o'clock at night. I do not think he really cared whether he lived or died, but when he made it across the pass and the road stretched before him, he turned off his lights. There was no one else on the road, and the forest loomed as it had on either side. Even by moonlight, the darkness was greater than he had remembered, and the loneliness more oppressive. But by this time all that mattered was to match the earlier feat.

What was going on here? It would be a mistake to think that this man wanted to forget his wife. The sheer weight of sorrow demanded that he distance himself for a time from her. It was as if all the photographs and the albums had to be put away for a while and the clocked turned back: "This never happened to me. I must pretend I never met her." But the way he told me the story suggests that something about that night journey made it possible for him to face his grief and keep living. I imagine it was very important to reclaim the young man who took a stretch of the back road to Klamath Falls without lights. It may have been just as important to say, "I can move forward by my own lights—I don't need your help." But as he tells it, that's not how it happened. As he crawled along the road, terrified of oncoming trucks and cars and traffic coming up behind him, he prayed to God and to his wife that they would keep him safe. In that moment, as he told it, the panic subsided, and he became aware of the deep silence and peace that had touched him so many years ago. He stopped for a while, turned on his headlights, and drove safely to Klamath Falls.

What does this story teach us? I do not presume to speak for the original teller. His lightless journeys across the mountains have meanings for him that we cannot begin to fathom. Two things are clear for me, however. First, he repeats the journey because he needs to reclaim who he was before he met his wife. But, second, the repeat journey reveals his dependence on his deceased wife. He is frightened to be on a lonely road without his lights on (but at the same time determined not to turn them on), and prays to God and to his wife to guide him. Are they being asked to keep him safe with his lights off, or to tell him to turn his lights on? I don't know. Would his wife have approved of him continuing down the highway with his lights off? I doubt it. But something beyond highway safety is at issue here. This man is facing a future in a world without his wife, and the question for him is whether that world is an enemy or a friend. Does the moon spell menace or guardianship? Do the towering trees welcome us or ward us off?

The answer for this man was peace. When he prayed to God and to his wife (I suspect that the prayer to God was incidental), he learned that there was nothing in the universe that was his enemy.

I doubt he could have taken in this message without the years spent with his wife, who (whatever fears she herself was struggling with) would have represented for him the challenge to give himself over in trust to something larger than himself. I imagine him in the middle of nowhere, the engine off, the wind hissing through the ponderosas, the deer just out of sight, the moon bearing down. He realizes that the original dare—"Can I make it through this no-man's-land as if on horseback?"—has been transformed into an acceptance: "I thank you for the gift of life in a world we are meant not just to travel through but to befriend."

1. What losses do you carry with you? In what ways do they affect your relationship with your beloved? For example, if your mother died when you were young, do you carry with you a great fear of loss of your partner now? Can you name these losses to your partner, and perhaps work with her or him to find healing that will bring a further wholeness to your relationship now?

2. How do you want your partner to approach her life after your death? What do you hope for your partner in this situation? Yes, it is difficult to imagine parting when at the beginning of your life together, but loss sometimes takes us by surprise, and if you are clear with your partner now, he will not need to wonder what you would think when it is too late to ask.

3. The nitty-gritty of death is something few wish to talk about, but it is as important to discuss now as it is to discuss children, finances, and the mission of your household. Discuss with your partner how and where you wish to be buried. Recognize that this can and will change over the years, but establish now a pattern of openness about this, so that no one is rushed to a decision at a time when decision-making is most difficult.

Exercise:

Each of you, write a letter to your beloved, saying what you want him or her to know after you have parted. Keep the letters together in a place you both know, but keep the contents private. Return to them once every few years and update them. Then, when you and your partner part—whether through death or dissolution of the relationship—read the letter your partner wrote. If the parting is through death, know that this letter contains an ongoing source of love and hopefully a source of healing for you, the partner left behind. If the parting is through the dissolution of the relationship, each of you can read the other's letter when you are ready, and will hopefully be able to celebrate the relationship you once had with this person you loved, for the dissolution of the relationship in no way negates the love you once had for each other.

TEN

Epilogue
Finding a Community of Faith

SO FAR WE HAVE BEEN UNPACKING THE SANCTITY OF SACRED unions by appreciating and exploring what it means to intend life-long union. It's the total self-giving that makes a union sacred. But there is another element that makes for sanctity, which has been implicit throughout this discussion: being accountable to a larger fellowship—not just any fellowship, but one that also aspires to faithfulness.

If sacred unions provide the opportunity to practice love of neighbor, then they require the support of a faith community that understands this project and is committed to it. Such a community will include other partnered couples, but it will also include single people, some of whom hope to enter into a sacred union, some of whom are called to serve the neighbor out of their singleness.

Anyone, in any condition or stage of life, who is devoted to the love of neighbor and who is trying to live that out faithfully, is a source of strength and inspiration for a couple walking down the path of lifelong union. But when like-minded disciples of neighbor-love are bound together—however loosely—in the bond of mutual recognition and mutual accountability, then the strength and vision offered to a couple is incomparably greater.

A Place of Refuge

In his book *Living Buddha, Living Christ*,[12] Thich Nhat Hanh speaks of the *sangha,* the community of people seeking to follow the teachings of Buddha. He reminds us that in Buddhism the sangha is one of the three things in which refuge can be taken (the others are dharma, or the teachings of Buddhism, and the Buddha himself). Buddhism may require the practice of solitude for some, but at the deepest level you cannot be a Buddhist by yourself, even when you are alone. The spiritual journey requires companions, cheerleaders, friends who will listen and give good counsel. What Thich Nhat Hanh is saying about the sangha is true about the Church as well. As he says, the Church is a kind of sangha, one that offers anyone who is trying to follow Jesus a refuge from a world that is often indifferent to the way of the cross (or the dharma, or any coherent and costly path toward love). I would add that for Christians the Church is a critical component of the spiritual journey because, like sacred unions, it is practice for the kingdom of God. If sacred unions provide intense practice one-on-one, the Church provides a more diffuse but on balance no less significant preparation for the widespread fellowship we can expect in heaven.

Stumbling Toward the Way of the Cross

It makes sense, then, that a couple embarking on life together would either be grounded in a faith community or be looking for one. But very often this is not the case. Two people meet, they fall in love, they give themselves to each other unreservedly, and they genuinely intend permanent fidelity—all this without the help of any religious teaching or practice.

This constantly amazes me. I am not astonished by the lack of any religious practice—that is common enough these days. What fills me with wonder is the readiness of such couples to place themselves under the discipline of permanent monogamy without any over-whelming external pressure to do so.

Is this just an example of the kind of self-absorption that gives romanticism a bad name? I don't think so. The churchless couples I frequently counsel have no interest in barricading themselves against the world. They want to establish households and take their place in the world.

Is this just the afterglow of a time when marriage was assumed and everything else followed? Perhaps. But there is more to it than that. We must keep in mind that true love is a form of the love of neighbor, whether or not it emerges in the context of religious faith. So we should not be surprised to find any true lover catapulted out of his self-centeredness into sheer awareness of the beloved as sepa-rate, mysterious, beyond reach. But, as we noticed earlier, this ori-entation outward takes in more than the beloved.

The true lover is awakened to the presence of every other neigh-bor as well. That is why the arts constantly depict love as a state marked by a heightened awareness of the human scene—children playing in the schoolyard, the homeless man pushing his cart full of empty cans, the old woman leaning out to water the flowerpots. True love is never oriented inward. Its whole direction is at one and the same time outward to the beloved, and outward into the world in which the beloved stands.

So from a Christian perspective, true lovers have always already stumbled onto the way of the cross, which is nothing other than a path of increasing openness to other people. The lovers may not be sure what this way means, or where it leads, but they know that the integrity of their relationship depends on their continued movement in the direction outward on which their love has set them.

This describes a number of the couples I have joined together in the University Chapel. When they ask me or one of my associ-ates to officiate at their ceremony, it is usually because they do not belong to a community of faith and have no clergyperson they can call on. I find, however, that they are more than ready to explore the spiritual implications of their commitment, and that the religious language of the service provides words and a frame of reference for what they are already going through. When I counsel such couples, I encourage them to talk about their faith—and their questions about faith—and I encourage them to identify a church that can be a sangha for them.

Church in the Public Square

But if the church is a refuge, it can also be a place of exposure. That is because churches are essentially public institutions. They do not belong to the public sector—at least not in any country that separates church from state—but they inhabit the public square. Christian worship is by its very nature a public act, since it is a witness to all and it is open to all. After all, Christianity is ultimately about being visible in the world, not hidden. We are not a secret society.

Church is also the place where the practical social and political implications of faith are articulated and explored. There are certainly churchgoers who think topics like war or economic justice should be avoided in the pulpit, but this is because they misconstrue the kind of refuge it is appropriate to find in church. Church is a refuge from indifference and the avoidance of religion. It is no refuge from the challenges and difficult choices any religious faith is sure to face us with. Because the doors of the church are necessarily open to everyone, church is—or should be—an occasion to encounter the stranger, and to share the event of worship—one of the most personal and exposing activities one can engage in—with people who are very different from oneself.

Finally, it must be acknowledged that church can sometimes be acrimonious. This is true in every tradition and every denomination I know of. This should come as no surprise, since congregational life attracts people with such differing convictions and then draws those convictions to the surface by encouraging us to relate how we live and how we vote to what we believe. It is true that most congregations tend to become homogenous in one respect or another—race, income, politics—but no group of people is ever too like-minded to have nothing to argue about.

Most of us avoid seeing the Church in this light, but it is important not to soft-pedal the existence of Church fights. Too many people leave the Church after their first experience of a contentious meeting. If they had entered the community with their eyes open, their faith in the Church might not have been so shaken. To decry the fact that people behave badly even—or especially—in church is to wish away the very point of the church as a moral practice. As I suggested above, Church trains us for the Kingdom. It does this by drawing us into close proximity and making us learn how to love one another despite our differences. It is also important to remember that the relationship of a couple to a congregation is a two-way street. Covenanted couples need the congregation to be supportive, and they depend on it as a source of accountability. But congregations also depend on the gifts and the witness of their members to support the whole body in its struggle to be faithful and generous. Covenanted couples who have weathered their own bouts of disagreement and acrimony have much to offer the entire assembly by way of wisdom, encouragement, and the modeling of mutual respect—if they will only offer it by sticking out the tough times and being a force for peace. Remaining faithful to congregational life even when that life seems unhealthy or hard-hearted is one of the most powerful ways a couple can live out its own covenant for the world's sake.

So when I urge couples to find a church home if they don't already have one, I am careful to stress that there is no congregation where they will not encounter normal human unpleasantness at some point. But I will also say here what I say in premarital counseling: the benefits of being part of a community of faith far outweigh the costs. The smaller groupings that are the building blocks of congregational life—Bible study and prayer groups, choirs, social outreach committees—provide invaluable (and often otherwise rare) settings for a couple to engage *as a couple* with other people, and discover what their union uniquely contributes to the world. The ministry of Word and Sacrament, the cycle of festivals, and the opportunities for study all ensure that a couple's true love for each other becomes grounded in the story of God's true love for the human race. Again, a skilled pastor can be the difference between relational breakdown and renewal, if a couple will only confide their trouble before it's too late.

Finally, and perhaps most importantly, the public character of the church in all its aspects is a constant reminder of the whole human world as the field of God's working. By connecting us to the Church in all times and all places, the local congregation becomes the frontier that opens onto that terrain, and so goads us to keep moving outward toward the neighbor.

I conclude by inviting you, as a couple, to begin a journey to find your refuge-that-exposes. It may mean you will visit several faith communities, perhaps several faith traditions, before you find yourselves drawn to a particular group of people. How will you know which is the one for you? When you both feel the impulse to look away from each other and toward the community gathered around you. That is the sign of the place where your true love will grow to know and represent the fullness of God's love for the world.

Notes

1. See, for instance, James McClendon's discussion in *Systematic Theology: Ethics* (Nashville: Abingdon Press, 2002), 133–155. I agree with McClendon's rejection of a cult of romantic love that is essentially selfish and self-absorbed. I am also indebted to him for his contribution toward the recovery of a Christian romanticism, although I go further than he is willing to go in associating that tradition with the poetry of the troubadours and their spiritual descendants.

2. See *City of God* 19:17. For the early Augustine on this point, see *On Christian Doctrine* 1:22.

3. For an opposing view, see Denis de Rougemont, *Love in the Western World* (Princeton, NJ: Princeton University Press, 1983).

4. From "Twelve Songs" in W. H. Auden, *Collected Poems* (New York: Random House, 1976), 120.

5. This episode takes up the last two cantos of Book 3 of *The Faerie Queene,* the "Legend of Chastity."

6. *Summa Theologiae: A Concise Translation,* ed. Timothy McDermott (Allen, TX: Christian Classics, 1991), 516.

7. See the second-century Christian book *The Shepherd of Hermas,* which was enormously popular in the early Church and was granted the authority of scripture by some. In his second "similitude," the author compares the poor to the elm, which bears no fruit (that is, they are not economically productive), while the rich are compared to the grapevine, which, although it produces much fruit, depends on the elm to prop it up. In other words, the poor are materially dependent on the rich, but the rich are spiritually dependent on the poor. See Bart D. Ehrman, ed. and trans., *The Apostolic Fathers II: Epistle of Barnabas. Papias and*

Quadratus. Epistle to Diogenetus. The Shepherd of Hermas. Loeb Classical Library (Cambridge, MA: Harvard University Press, 2003).

8. The quotation is from Wesley's sermon "The Use of Money," reproduced in *On Moral Business: Classical and Contemporary Resources for Ethics in Economic Life,* Max L. Stackhouse *et al.,* eds. (Grand Rapids, MI: Eerdmans, 1995), 194–197.

9. See Gregory of Nyssa, *On Virginity,* in *Nicene and Post-Nicene Fathers,* vol. 5, eds. P. Schaff and H. Wace (Peabody, MA: Hendrickson Publishers, 1995), 343–371. For Augustine, see *On the Good of Marriage,* in volume 3 of the same series, 397–413.

10. Hannah Arendt, *The Human Condition* (Chicago: University of Chicago Press, 1958), 235–236.

11. See Luther's "The Freedom of a Christian," in *Three Treatises* (Minneapolis: Fortress Press, 1970), 284: "Just as the heated iron glows like fire because of the union of fire with it, so the Word imparts its qualities to the soul."

12. Published by Riverhead Books, New York, 1995. See especially pages 63–66.